The Once and Future Parish

Alison Milbank

scm press

© Alison Milbank 2023

Published in 2023 by SCM Press
Editorial office
3rd Floor, Invicta House,
108–114 Golden Lane,
London EC1Y 0TG, UK

www.scmpress.co.uk

SCM Press is an imprint of Hymns Ancient & Modern Ltd
(a registered charity)

Hymns Ancient & Modern® is a registered trademark of
Hymns Ancient & Modern Ltd
13A Hellesdon Park Road, Norwich,
Norfolk NR6 5DR, UK

British Library Cataloguing in Publication data

A catalogue record for this book is available
from the British Library

978-0-334-06313-1

Typeset by Regent Typesetting
Printed and bound in Great Britain by
CPI Group (UK) Ltd

Contents

Though for no other cause, yet for this; that posterity may know we have not loosely through silence permitted things to pass away as in a dream, there shall be for men's information extant thus much concerning the present state of the Church of God established amongst us, and their careful endeavour which would have upheld the same.

Richard Hooker, Preface to *Of the Laws of Ecclesiastical Polity*

Acknowledgements

I should like to thank everyone who patiently answered my questions about their parishes and gave me details of the excellent work going on in local churches, especially the Reverends Johannes Arens, Campbell Paget and Darren Percival. The seminar participants in the Edward King Centre course on themes from this book also offered valuable insights, and I am grateful to St Stephen's House, Oxford, and to Fr Andreas Wenzel for the opportunity to give this course. This book would have been impossible without the inspiration of the Revd Marcus Walker and the members of the Steering Committee of Save the Parish. I should stress, however, that what is argued in this book represents my own views and not those of Save the Parish or of Andrew Davison. We all owe a debt to the Financial Scrutiny Group of STP, who have done painstaking professional study of diocesan accounts hitherto never attempted. My thanks are due to Stephen Billyeald and Andrew Orange for corrections to Chapter 3. Paul Avis and Colin Podmore generously answered queries about episcopacy. Peter Howson generously gave permission to reproduce his painting, *Theophania*

I would also like to thank those who have read drafts of other chapters or the whole book: Andrew Davison, Arabella Milbank Robinson, John Milbank, James Robinson and Emma Thompson. I am grateful to Mary Matthews for seeing the book through production and to the meticulous work of Christopher Pipe in copy-editing the manuscript and compiling the index. Finally, I am indebted to my editor David Shervington, who has been so patient during the gestation of this study, and to SCM Press for supporting a follow-up to *For the Parish*.

Figure 1: Peter Howson, *Theophania*, 2020, mixed media.

This book is dedicated to the memory of
two faithful parish priests:

John Suddards, vicar of St Mary's, Thornbury,
who was murdered in 2012.

David Scott, poet, former vicar of St Lawrence's,
Winchester, who died in 2022.

May they rest in peace and rise in glory.

Introduction
For the Parish Twelve Years On

The illustration on page xi, from a work by Glasgow artist Peter Howson, is a shocking image, typical of this painter of the marginal, who has faced his own demons. Bodies writhe towards the light, with terrifying monsters peering from beneath them. A knowing skull peers out at the viewer from the foreground, while tendrils of bulbous viruses extrude from the drains. This is a painting from Howson's *Lockdown* series and the marks of the coronavirus are everywhere, pimpling the surface. Yet Howson's illustration is not merely a representation of attack by disease, but expresses a wider critique of our culture, with Vanity Fair held in the taloned grip of a demonic figure. He shows us a world of chaos and conflict worthy of the book of Revelation, in which a battle in the skies is under way, emblematic of the war in heaven between Michael and the dragon in Revelation 17.

This painting embodies the sense of crisis that drives the writing of this book, which is, of course, global in nature. We are still, as I write, riven with cases of coronavirus, with the consequent effects on our health and public services, which are straining at the seams. Inflation is rising apace, with energy costs prohibitive for poorer people, and every sign that this will worsen. As I write, war in Ukraine continues with no end in sight, but possible escalation. Meanwhile, global temperatures continue to rise, the number of living species shrinks and there is little evidence that we have done enough to address our environmental crisis.

One of the most chilling elements in all this is the dearth of moral leadership, which would enable us to think collectively in terms of the Common Good about our situation. All the more, then, do we need prophetic artists such as Peter Howson to show us our need. A Christian, whose faith saved him in his alcoholic addiction, Howson is trenchant about the heart of our troubles: 'We are decadent in the West and have lost the ability to really change. We are losing our religion and idolizing our humanity – which is always a mistake.'[1]

His painting is, however, called, *Theophania*, Theophany, or divine manifestation. It embodies Howson's belief that 'we should all be turning to God. That is our only answer.'[2]

The picture offers resources to address the human needs identified. Amid the swirling wreckage is the Bible and a copy of the works of the early Christian writer Origen of Alexandria. Origen looked to the restoration of all things in God and believed that all people and all creatures would eventually be saved from sin and perishing. His is a hopeful and inclusive theology. So, in the painting, nearly all the needy human figures are reaching towards the central figure, who may be Christ himself, God with us. One book in the picture bears the legend 'Jesus wept' from John 11.35, suggesting the sympathetic presence of Christ amid the distress and suffering.

To the upper left and right of the painting are manifestations of the divine grace: one from the stars and the other from a lighthouse-cum church. It was this latter image that prompted me to use Howson's painting, for it shows faith in the traditional Church as a source of help and inspiration in dark times. This book is a plea to fellow Anglicans to recognize the parish system as a key asset in addressing the massive challenges that face us. The parish church is today vulnerable and small, endangered and regarded as a thing of the past by so many of our leaders and yet its potential is enormous and has something to offer to every one of the contemporary problems with which we have to deal.

Theophania reveals the divine nature of the Church as truly salvific. For the ship from which the central figures emerge is itself called *Theophania* and is very much the ecclesial vessel.

The miner with his lamp suggests the Holy Spirit, who is closely connected by the light beam with the little church, while the two large human figures suggest God the Father and the Son. On another level, they might be Dante and his guide Virgil crossing the River Styx in Hell, which may become Purgatorial reconciliation under the optimistic theology of Origen. A second name given for the ship is Beatrice, the woman whose spiritual power and beauty led Dante through Paradise to a vision of the divine Trinity. Such an analogy suggests that the divine presence is manifest in you and me: that human followers of Christ can be his image-bearers and bring light and love to the world. And note how ready so many of the human figures in the painting are to receive life and healing as they turn yearningly towards the central figure.

This is a painting that looks to the Church as the ark to save people for Christ and celebrates the inclusivity of the parish church. Yet this confidence in our traditional faith and practices is not mirrored in the official policy documents and strategy of the Anglican Church today, just as it was already being undermined in the report *Mission-Shaped Church* of 2004, to which Andrew Davison and I responded in the book *For the Parish: A Critique of Fresh Expressions*, to which this book is a sequel and update. We wrote:

> This book is written in the belief that an important choice is offered to the Church of England: to embrace her historic mission to evangelize and serve the whole people of this country, or to decline into a sect.[3]

This choice is now much more pressing, and it may already be too late, since once patterns of behaviour and belief generations old are disturbed, they are hard to re-establish, as Covid-19 and its aftermath have shown us.

In *For the Parish*, we launched a strong critique of the way Fresh Expressions was conceived in relation to Church tradition, doctrine and Christian anthropology. In no way were we averse to evangelism, but we saw in the individualistic and choice-driven model a challenge to our whole Anglican life and practice, and a project that would divide the parish from the mission initiative in ways that would be destructive to our unity and, indeed, our effectiveness. Much of the theological groundwork was laid in the earlier book, so that this is a more polemical essay, but one that is offered to the Church that I love in the hope that there is a growing consensus that we need to rescue the Church of England from herself. For the astonishing early success of the 'Save the Parish' movement has shown me that there is a groundswell of concern behind me among the diverse people of England, especially ordinary lay Anglicans. Moreover, this threat to the parish also resonates way beyond the pews and is drawing non-believers to see its value.

Some of our argument in *For the Parish* was specific to the Fresh Expressions idea, in which people were to be evangelized in networks and specific identities, so that one might have a church of surfboarders, knitters or bikers. We spent a great deal of time patiently demonstrating that how we do something embodies what we are communicating – form and content cohere – as well as attacking the choice-driven individualist anthropology as a potential model for what it is to be the Church. Yet although Fresh Expressions is still official policy, it has morphed so as to represent any new worshipping community and is primarily locally situated. Ironically, many of what passes for the 2,000 Fresh Expressions still going strong are the parish-led Messy Churches, which are in essence creatively updated Sunday Schools. Like so many initiatives in a Church that is ever creating more reports and projects, Fresh Expressions in its pure ideological form is a thing of the past.

However, the other arguments in our book about the flight from tradition and the turning away from inclusivity towards segregation and a gathered church are more apposite than ever, and I shall refer back to them when we examine the nature of the new 'resource' churches and how they often fail to do the hard work of the parish to behave, indeed, like Anglican churches in any recognizable form. Moreover, the dearth of any ecclesiological reflection has become ever more acute and our analysis of the role of mediation in Christian negotiation with culture takes on increased relevance in a time in which the

Church and society are facing newly vocal cries for justice by our Christian brothers and sisters of colour.

For the Parish made something of a splash, both positively and negatively, and was one of the books that prompted the report *Fresh Expressions in the Mission of the Church*, with some broadly sympathetic readers believing we had a point but were over-reacting. In the years since we wrote, however, all our fears have been realized, especially in the way huge amounts of money have been poured into mission initiatives that compromise and rival the parish system, to little appreciable benefit. The Chote Report of 2022, for example, noted that of the 89,375 new disciples promised in Strategic Development Funding projects from 2014–21, only 12,705 had been 'witnessed'.[4]

The kind of competitive bidding characteristic of Private Finance Initiatives in public services has been introduced to endow 'resource' churches with multiple ministers, while local parish clergy struggle with ever more churches to serve, and small or rural churches are in many places ruled out as bidders for this SDF from the start. In response to criticisms of this fact, the latest triennial budget has increased such funding and opened it to all parishes, but the competitive principle remains. Few rural churches would have the resources or expertise to apply, even if they could gain the necessary diocesan backing.

Not only has this competitive bidding damaged local church relations, but while fewer parish clergy care for ever more congregations, especially in rural areas, the number of people employed by diocesan structures has grown exponentially, as I shall later demonstrate. Indeed, rather than become a simpler Church, as *Vision and Strategy* claims is one key aim, this dual system of parish and New Worshipping Community or Resource Church creates ever more layers of bureaucracy, as does the cruel reorganization of parishes into huge megaparishes or 'mission areas' with a taxi-rank system for occasional offices such as baptisms and funerals. Rather than resisting the pressures towards managerialism in society at large, the Church has embraced them, and now offers a queasy mixture of missiology and management-speak in every report, with very little evidence of theological analysis of the management techniques employed.

All this centralized diocesan and national control is expensive, so that the pecuniary demands on declining congregations are increased at the very time in which less of diocesan money is spent on stipends for clergy and the meagre clerical provision parishes enjoy grows ever more vestigial. Add to this the great number of historic and often ancient buildings to maintain with no state support, and one can appreciate the enormous strain all this places on Parochial Church Councils and Churchwardens, who must raise ever more money to receive less in return.

No wonder then that a movement like Save the Parish is a primarily laity-driven organization, a revolt at long last by the 'people of England'. It feels to so many of those faithful Anglicans as if they are forsaken by the Church and not valued. Even the Archbishops realize that 'there is a lack of trust', prompting the Archbishop of York to invite himself to the Save the Parish summer conference in 2022, not even a year after its inception. Rather than being 'set free' as yet another report has it, the laity feel constrained and yet abandoned. What will be left of the forty per cent of Anglicans who live in rural areas when cure of souls is wholly vestigial in megaparishes of twenty or so churches? The Church Commissioners' own green paper, *Mission in Revision*, aptly nicknamed the 'Church Closers' Charter', reports that in Wales, where this policy has been implemented everywhere, 'anecdotal evidence ... suggests a super-parish type model has not worked well'.[5]

Clergy similarly lost their trust during the coronavirus lockdown period of 2020, when the archbishops denied them access to their churches and did not address at any point the fact that they were asking clergy to break canon law in so doing. According to its rubrics, an incumbent must enter his or her church each morning, ring the bell and say Morning Prayer. No one would have been put at risk had clergy been allowed to carry on, and yet their own mental and spiritual health was put at risk by the ban. One colleague told me he just stood outside his church building and rested his hand on the stone to gain some consolation and stability.

The trust of clergy was also lost by the report by Madeleine Davies in the *Church Times* of a Gregory Centre for Church Multiplication conference in 2021, at which the unfortunate John McGinley was quoted as saying that 'lay-led churches release the church from key limiting factors', which he named as 'a building and a stipend and long costly college-based training for every leader of a church'.[6] He also referred to 10,000 new lay-led churches, which confused everyone as sounding like the 10,000 new congregations the Church of England was planning. McGinley spoke at a semi-official event rife with episcopal purple in a seminar shared with the Bishop at Lambeth, but no evidence has been adduced that the bishop questioned this negative presentation of the stipendiary clergy. It seemed from all this as if lay-led churches were being introduced under the rose, against all Anglican ecclesial order or tradition.

And yet this was very much part of the vision of the Archbishops' Renewal and Reform programme, outlined in 2015, which placed mission and growth at the centre of all ecclesial activity, and actively promoted lay-led ministry. Leicester Diocese's reorganization plans in 2021 even allowed for a lay person holding the cure of souls in the new mission communities, until an amendment passed at the diocesan synod disallowed it.

Outside the Anglican twitter-sphere, clergy are much more reticent than laity about their disquiet and one reason for this, for which I have considerable evidence, is fear. Martyn Percy has described what is afoot in the Church of England as akin to the Great Leap Forward of Maoist China: 'It was not good enough to profess to be a good Communist and loyal Chinese citizen. Chinese Communism was turned into a cult of personality followership: to survive and prosper, you had to demonstrate that you were *a loyal disciple* of Mao.'[7] Comparing the episcopal bench to the Chinese Politburo might seem extreme, but the latest iteration of Church policy, *Vision and Strategy*, is to be accepted as dogma, despite the dearth of discussion and debate, and the fact that General Synod was required to do nothing but 'welcome' it.

In a climate of church reorganization and loss of posts – Chelmsford alone planned to lose 60 posts by 2022 – it is a rare cleric who can stand up and question the whole basis of Church policy. Only because the Church does not pay me can I afford to be as forthright as this and to speak on behalf of those who cannot. Moreover, it is understandable that if you are a priest in a diocese that seems to have no other recourse than to merge churches, you will often see no alternative and have, perhaps, a somewhat jaundiced view of the sustainability of your own parishes. You might see the problems and the complexity of the situation but find it hard to step back and look creatively at alternative options.

I do not believe that our leaders are malign, but that they have lost faith in their own traditions, of which much more later. They too are fearful, I believe, and are anxious that the whole Church of England will take no Great Leap Forward, but rather go down the plughole to which the *Vision and Strategy* diagram has been compared.[8] Naturally, they do not really want to see the ship sink under their watch and they will do anything that they believe will right the vessel and allow her to sail into the future. Because a large number of parishes are declining in numbers, they can see no future for them and have mistakenly decided that an alternative, non-parish solution can keep the vessel afloat.

Unfortunately, therefore, despite their frequent protestations to the contrary, our leaders have truly given up on the parish as having any role in the Church's navigation of the future. They look at the often-elderly worshippers in the pews and discount them. Parish is just 'inherited church' and has had its day. At the launch of 'Save the Parish' in July 2021, I suggested they saw the parochial system as a rather embarrassing heirloom left by a great aunt which they would really prefer to consign to the attic. For Andrew Davison and me in *For the Parish*, this fact was evident all those years ago and we spoke boldly to the contrary: that the parish is a flexible institution and as much the key to our future as to our past, since it holds an inexhaustible richness of resource. Books following ours, such as Andrew Rumsey's *Parish* have demonstrated the philosophical, theological, ecological 'fit' of the parish and the sense of place to our embodiment and our salvation. There is also David Brown's pan-sacramental *God and Enchantment of Place*, John Inge's *A Christian Theology of Place* and Ben Quash's *Abiding*, to name but a few titles. Moreover, as we shall see, the secular ecological movement has embraced the parochial ideal. Nothing comparable can be found on the other side of the argument, with little attempt to ground the new missiology and ecclesiology philosophically.

This brief sketch is an attempt to highlight some of the key issues that now face the Church of England some years on from *For the Parish*, and which will be discussed in more detail in later chapters: the turn away from an inclusive to a gathered church model, the loss of confidence in Anglican orders, liturgy and doctrine, especially ecclesiology, the embrace of managerialism and centralized bureaucracy; the whole movement of attention and money away from parochial models of mission to functional ones.

What I shall be urging is a change of course before it is finally too late, in which we renew our commitment to Anglican orders, liturgy and the inclusivity of the parish, and put resources behind that confidence. I shall offer an alternative narrative which seeks to make sense of the current factors driving us and the financial and policy decisions that have led us to the brink of disaster. Building upon that, I shall seek to demonstrate the potential that still lies in the parish in a time of global environmental crisis and rising costs of living. At Bethel, Jacob woke from his sleep and said, 'Surely the LORD is in this place – and I did not know it!' (Gen. 28.16). It is time for all people of good will to wake up to the truth that although our parish churches are going through lean times, they are our social bedrock, and it is only when we embrace the givenness of the local riches with which God has endowed us that we can dream new and sustainable visions for the future.

To return to Peter Howson's *Theophania*: notice the raven perched on the side of the ship. Biblically, the raven is always the sign of God's provision for us, as when he sent the ravens to feed the prophet Elijah. Christ urged us: 'Consider the ravens: They do not sow or reap, they have no storeroom or barn; yet God feeds them' (Luke 12.24). We need to craft a mission strategy that is based on trust in God's prevenient grace rather than lack or panic. The parish is our most ancient British institution, which has changed and developed over many centuries, and it has treasures old and new to produce. This book is entitled *The Once and Future Parish* in imitation of the folk-lore hero, King Arthur, the 'once and future king' who did not die but was taken to the Isle of Avalon to be healed, until the need of Britain was so great that he would return, to come to her rescue.[9] Another legend has it that Arthur was transformed into a raven, so that the quizzical friendly bird in Howson's image may hint at the Arthurian hope. It is so easy to consign the parish to the past, as an idea that has had its day, and those standing up for it as nostalgic. I hope to demonstrate that there is a future parish because a world of ecological emergency and increasing localism will demand it as a sign of *theophania*, God's presence in our midst, calling us beyond our fears to reimagine community together, as a place of holiness and reconciliation, worthy of Christ, the true once and future king.

National Mission and Local Embodiment

What is the Church of England? The distinguished ecclesiastical historian Jeremy Morris has answered that question by the title of his recent book on this very topic, *A People's Church*.[1] One's first thought might be surprise, given the difficulty the Church has had attracting the urban working-class, for example, and the recent census figures, which show a minority of the population owning allegiance to Christianity. The point that Morris is making, however, is that until very recently it would have been 'common sense' to people of this nation to view their existence through the Christian Church, which formed 'the overarching framework in which they interpreted the world'.[2] That is not to say that there were not changes, some of them extreme, in the understanding of that faith and its practice over the centuries. But a contrasting and real continuity lies in the assumption that the Church of England is the Church *for* England and its people, which goes back to at least the Venerable Bede in the eighth century writing his *Ecclesiastical History of the English People*. The intention is clear, to give an account of a church for the whole people.

The way this national vision has been embodied is through the parish, where establishment is expressed in local form. Morris chides Anglicans for thinking it is their particular mode of organization, pointing out that it is a practically universal institution.[3] The value of the parish is attested by the fact that Lutherans and Presbyterians as well as continental Catholics share it, while Anglican missionaries like the Cowley Fathers of the Society of St John the Evangelist founded parishes wherever they went in Africa or India. Writing after the French Revolution, the radical William Cobbett saw great value in the parish and its clergy as unifying factors precisely because of their local presence:

> The clergy are less powerful from their rank and industry than from their locality ... and their aggregate influence is astonishingly great. When from the top of any high hill, one looks around the country, and sees the multitude of regularly distributed spires, one ... ceases to wonder that order and religion are maintained. It is the equal distribution of the clergy, their being in every corner of the kingdom that makes them a powerful and formidable corps.[4]

The parish goes right back to the second century or before, when the bishop's Eucharist in the main city was too far away for those out in the villages and hamlets to reach.[5] It has been a geographical unit from the beginning. Nicholas Orme points out that the parish is a lay development, so that a church was often built by a local landowner for his family and employees as people settled into larger villages or hamlets.[6] Soon, a network of small parishes took the place of the large missionary minsters and from the tenth century onwards, completed by the twelfth, the whole land was parochially organized. Andrew Rumsey's theological and historical study of the parish notes how one cannot separate national from ecclesial organization in the founding of the territorial divisions of parish, diocese and province in Britain. Indeed, the ecclesial half creates the national identity, so that to be English is to belong to the Church of the English.[7]

The Reformation did nothing to disturb this parochial arrangement and actually reinforced it by making it a legal obligation to attend church on Sunday and by organizing poor-relief through the parishes, now that the monastic houses with their hospitals and charities had been dissolved. Cranmer's Book of Common Prayer went through various revisions but was established as the one book for public worship for four centuries (apart from the gap during the Commonwealth) and this book too was a highly unifying factor, linking local church to its national mission. In lockdown, during the Covid-19 epidemic, a rural parish church in Gloucestershire livestreamed its BCP Morning Prayer and found, to its members' amazement, that it was attended by thousands; in times of need, the traditional Prayer Book still has the potential to play a unifying, national role.

When Reformation theologians began to reflect upon what it meant to be the Church of England, they assumed this national mission and ancient foundation. This is clear in the earliest such attempt, John Jewel's *Apology for the Anglican Church* (*Ecclesiae Anglicanae*) of 1562, which sought to defend the Elizabethan settlement and establish that the Church of England is the true ancient Church of this island, while attacking the Church of Rome as corrupt and tyrannical. Protestant historiographers such as John Foxe and Archbishop Ussher made similar claims that it 'was no new begun matter, but even the old continued church', though 'of late years repressed by the tyranny of Romish bishops'.[8] Linkage back to the early church was an essential element of ecclesiology, because while *sola scriptura* (scripture alone) was the rallying cry of authority for the radical reformers, tradition remained highly important for the Protestant mainstream: God was at work in all of history, which was read through the lens of the book of Revelation. The Reformation historians lifted the veil of historical event to reveal God at work, and they saw the medieval period as the rule of Satan, with God's purposes being eschatologically fulfilled in their own day through the downfall of the Roman system.

The Church and Participation

The Anglican tradition supports such an ecclesiology in the magisterial work of Richard Hooker at the end of the sixteenth century, who, above all others, grounded Anglican ecclesiology in the whole tradition. Influenced both by the humanism of Philip Melanchthon (Luther's successor who turned towards a more generous and positive anthropology) but even more by the early Christian theologians and Thomas Aquinas, Hooker evolved what was later described as a 'middle way' between Catholicism and Reform Protestantism. Like Bede, he assumed a continuity between the polity and the Church, making an argument in favour of national churches, but grounded his understanding of the Church in its participation in God.

This is an emphasis particularly strong in eastern Christianity, which has a doctrine of *theosis,* whereby Christians are called to share in the life of God and to become divinized. For Hooker, such a path is effected through the sacramental life of baptism and Eucharist. Unlike many Protestants who, then as now, treat the Church as a human institution, it is for Hooker a divine society, the mystical union – 'inherent copulation' – of all those who have, are or will be joined to Christ in baptism (although offering hope also to those who might not have had the sacrament).[9] This includes Roman Catholics, in a gesture almost uniquely inclusive for that divisive time.

William Harrison points out that this emphasis on participation unites the visible church very closely to the mystical Jerusalem, as it is by way of the sacraments that we gain some of the benefits of the divine life. Through gradual sanctification under the operation of the Holy Spirit, we are increasingly incorporated into Christ's divine nature through the Church. The physicality of Hooker's prose makes the point:

> They that which belong to the mystical body of our Saviour Jesus Christ, and be in number as the stars of heaven, divided successively by reason of their mortal condition into many generations, are notwithstanding coupled everyone to Christ their Head, and all unto every particular person among themselves, inasmuch as the same Spirit, which anointed the blessed soul of our Saviour Christ, doth so formalize, unite and actuate his whole race, as if he and they were so many limbs compacted into one body, by being quickened all with one and the same soul.[10]

It is a language shared by the Book of Common Prayer, which speaks of Christians as 'very members incorporate in the mystical body' of Christ. It cannot be emphasized enough that this is the language of actual metaphysical incorporation and is not metaphorical, not one image among many that one might choose in order to describe the Church.[11]

When theologians are criticized for describing the Church in what are seen to be idealistic terms and accused of not recognizing the fallibility and failures of the members, their critics are not acknowledging this true nature of the Church as she really is, metaphysically speaking. Hooker, indeed, includes the erring and sinful explicitly, accepting that there are degrees of sanctification and that imperfection (which is not the same as evil) has its providential place.

We will not evangelize a secular world with a view of our members as irrelevant, or not true disciples. What will energize traditional Anglicans is a vision of their incorporation in the mystical body, which intensifies and renders theological the life they already understand as being in community. The fact that we are sinful creatures who fail in manifesting this vision is an impetus to recalling us to this truth and not a denial of it. Thus, to use human fallibility as an argument against the divine constitution and communion of the Church is to separate the human and divine natures of the Church as constituting Augustine's *Christus totus,* a move that Anglican ecclesiology throughout its history has resisted and which marks it out from more explicitly Protestant conceptions.[12]

In the comprehensive ecclesiology of the 'broad' nineteenth-century theologian F. D. Maurice, for example, the Church is presented as being herself a sacrament, a sign of the interdependence of humanity and its suspension from the divine. She is ultimately indefectible, yet constantly falls short. Maurice resolves this paradox in Hookerian terms by invoking the divine and human natures of Christ. As Jeremy Morris puts it:

> Just as Christ's will was united to that of the Father, yet subject to the full conditions of humanity, situated in history, and not intruded into it, so the Church in like manner, as the community inhabited by the Spirit, was united with the Son in its inner reality, yet again also fully embedded in history and subject to the constraining pressures of history.[13]

F. D. Maurice had such an inclusive vision of the Church that it was for him, in truth, the world itself as owning the Incarnation of Christ, which grounds every human relationship and social organization from the family to the nation: 'if Christ be really the head of every man, and if He really have taken human flesh, there is a ground for human fellowship among men ... Now the denial of a universal head is practically the denial of all communion in society.'[14]

Value of the Parish in the Oxford Movement and the Evangelical Revival

While Maurice's idea of national churches can be vulnerable to a nationalistic interpretation, his emphasis on the inter-personal values equally the familial and the local. Every level of relationship from the friend to the parish and the state is part of the 'sacred constitution'. Maurice himself was an example of someone who forged deep and generative relationships, so that his theology had a beneficial influence on the development of post-Tractarian thought. The early Oxford Movement, sig-nalled by a sermon by John Keble in response to what he saw as the subservience of the Church to the State, had been rightly anxious to stress the holiness and independent authority of the Church. It signalled a crisis in the confessional state, which would be repeated in the failure to pass the revision of the Book of Common Prayer through Parliament in 1927–28. But that the Oxford Movement became such a missionary force for renewal was partly due to the in-grafting of the incarnational theology and social inclusivity of Maurice's ecclesial vision, which united with it and bore fruit in later slum ritualism, Christian Socialism, and the whole incarnational theological project that marks high and broad-church Anglican theology to this day. This project tends to newly elevate the importance of the social, the artistic and the personally relational in the work of salvific transformation.

It is, however, important to note that evangelical ecclesiology in the late eighteenth and nineteenth century was also distinctly elevated in character. According to Peter Nockles, the apostolic succession was a generally held doctrine (with the exception of Whig ideologues) long before the Oxford Movement made it a central plank of their thinking.[15] Such a stress on sacramental continuity was of a piece with an historical understanding of the Church as a sacred transmission, which obtained among all sections of Anglicanism until recent times. Apostolic succession may be understood in different ways, but it speaks of a sustaining of tradition, biblical interpretation and doctrine, while acknowledging some sort of principle of development. In this context it is important to note that ever since Irenaeus and Hippolytus in the second and third centuries, apostolic succession has meant as much a faithfulness to teaching as it has the conveyance of a sacramental touching.

This period also witnessed a great revival in the clergy's understanding of their role as pastors with a cure of souls in their parish. To begin with, this was often the result of the evangelical revival. Charles Simeon, the famous vicar of Holy Trinity, Cambridge, for example, was an assiduous visitor of everyone in his parish, always asking: 'I am come to enquire about your welfare. Are you happy?'[16] He also faithfully visited the local prison and subsidized bakers to sell bread at prices local people could afford. Elisabeth Jay's study of Victorian evangelicalism points out that it was evangelicals who increased the frequency of Holy Communion services from quarterly to monthly and were assiduous in teaching the young their catechism from the Book of Common Prayer.[17] In this instance also Simeon is a good example. Not only was his own conversion prompted by his reception of the sacrament, but he loved the Anglican Prayer Book, saying, 'Never do I find myself nearer to God than I often am in the reading desk ... the finest sight short of heaven would be a whole congregation using the prayers of the Liturgy in the true spirit of them.'[18]

This revival of the pastoral and liturgical life of the parish after some eighteenth-century neglect was continued by the Tractarians. S. A. Skinner's study of the social and political concerns of the Oxford Movement argues 'that the locus of clerical government was to be the parish, whose functional autonomy was an antidote to the growth and pluralization of the state'.[19] Subsidiarity was the principle at work here and the relative autonomy of the parson in his freehold involved the exercise of a liberty now often denied to the Church at the state level. In the parish there should be a certain redistribution of wealth, from rich to poor, and spiritual equality should pertain within the church itself.

Hence the fierce campaign waged against *pews* by Tractarian priests, for what these meant at the time were a series of little private sections within the church, rented by the wealthy, with the poor excluded or pushed to the back. Thomas Keble, the brother of John, who became the ideal of the parish pastor for the early movement, was one of the first to attack the practice of pew-rents in his parish at Bisley, stopping up the thirteen separate entrances constructed by millowners to allow direct access to their private space.[20]

Pastoral care was at the heart of Tractarian ministry, again emphasizing the authority of the incumbent against secular authority, and his exercise of a holistic ministry. Keble was frequently ill from too often visiting sick parishioners, and he sponsored allotments and founded a parish savings bank.[21] Oxford Movement priests in urban parishes later earned respect by their pastoral care during cholera epidemics. Thomas Mozley looked back at his time in parish work with recollections that sum up the Tractarian attitude to parish ministry, which came to be shared widely by high, low and broad church people as the century progressed:

I had early cast in my lot with rural populations, lavishing upon them all I had of heart, mind, and worldly gear ... They were the only people I saw and talked with, and visited in their homes, seeing and hearing their troubles. Whatever had to be done for them beyond their scanty means and opportunities the parsonage had to do.[22]

The Parish after 1894

The establishment of the secular parish council in 1894 took over some of the parish's charitable and financial tasks and led to the foundation of the parochial church councils in 1921 as new versions of the old vestries. Yet the idea of the parish as territorial, as offering services, pastoral care and occasional offices to a local population persisted. And the Church of England still to this day claims to give a visible Christian presence in every community. The combination of the increased attention to Holy Communion by evangelicals with the emphasis on the Eucharist in the Oxford Movement has left its mark on most parishes where the Eucharist is the central service. They are equally marked by the revival of parish visiting and integral social care which both wings of the Church of England so signally encouraged. The incarnational co-belonging of liturgical celebration, social festivity and community outreach reached its apex in the Essex parish of Thaxted in the inter-war years, but this fusion had an almost universal influence, and its impact is still current in some inner-city parishes to this day, despite their often very different ethnic make-up.

It reached a more general culmination in the 'Indian summer' of Anglican revival after 1945, partly as an effect of the 'Parish and People' movement. That was a radical project of using the Eucharist as a tool of social transformation, whereby it was centred not so much on the individual 'making one's communion' as in the communal offering of the people of God. Sam Brewitt-Taylor has stressed its eschatological theology; but for many churches where it was practised, it represented a version of that same participatory, incarnational ecclesiology that I have been describing as a feature of Anglican thought since the late sixteenth century.[23] And it could see its celebration as inherently inclusive, for it was bringing the work, concerns and people of an entire parish to God for transformation. Still today, at St Lawrence Catford, they call their mission 'offering the prayer to God that Catford has forgotten'. The consecration of the particular that is involved here includes specific place as well as specific people, since nothing within either nature or culture lies outside the Divine Creation.

In 1967 Anglican evangelicals held an important conference at Keele University where they decided to leave their ghetto and engage more fully in Anglican life – indeed, to capture it. They pledged to be more socially involved, more ecumenical in spirit and to take the sacraments more seriously. On the Eucharist, the final statement read: 'We have failed to do justice in our practice to the twin truths that the Lord's Supper is the main service of the people of God, and that the local church, as such, is the unit within which it is properly ministered.'[24] The Congress admitted that Evangelicals had 'let the sacrament be pushed to the outer fringes of church life, and the ministry of the Word be divorced from it'. Nothing could more witness to the reality of an 'ecumenical Anglicanism' that is arguably more profound than its more evident divisions of belief and practice.

One could argue that it is social action, both individual and structural, that has been the mediating link between word and sacrament for both High and Low: a supremely meaningful personal performance. Although, in 1985, one theological college was already teaching that visiting was no longer a pastoral duty, it was certainly central to my own training incumbent's idea of ministry, even though he combined running a parish with a full-time senior diocesan role. We might not be like John Henry Newman, who got round his Littlemore households within two months of arrival, but the idea of George Herbert's country parson still energizes many who seek ordination, despite the warning of Justin Lewis-Anthony, who believes the Herbert ideal just sets clergy up to fail in today's church.[25] For clergy need not be on their own. In the past, churches like St John's Kennington relied on a body of parish visitors, who went visiting themselves from street to street throughout the parish and it was they who would alert clergy to particular needs and to those who needed a special pastoral visit.[26]

Indeed, the most positive development to come out of the recent Renewal and Reform series of initiatives is the Estates Evangelism Task Group, which was established in 2019 and which seeks to ensure a worshipping communal presence on every social housing estate in England through supporting already existing churches on these estates and planting new ones. This is an outworking of the national mission to provide a presence in every community and is in continuity with nineteenth-century Anglican parish outreach, such as that of Canon Jacobs in Leeds or the vast working-class parish of St Mary Portsea and its establishment of mission churches.

Sidelining the Parish Church

It is only in our day that ecclesiology is beginning to dissociate itself from territorial tradition: it did not begin with the action of the Reformers. One can nonetheless find echoes of their tendency at times unwarrantedly to deny many centuries of universal Christian tradition, in the report *Fresh Expressions in the Mission of the Church* (2012). It seeks to address the theological and ecclesiological vacuum of the earlier *Mission-Shaped Church*, by reading back the contemporary 'fresh expression' into the book of Acts with its 'loose-knit dynamic network' model contrasted to centralized authority.[27] This report seeks to ground an account of tradition in a dialogue between margins and centre, but although it purports to get to grips with Christian history, historical precedent is covertly bracketed, with the early Acts model alone privileged and this model itself implausibly presented as the contemporary 'mixed economy' of parish and 'fresh expression' network. It is implausible because all the evidence demonstrates that as far as one can contextualize worship in the first century, it was locally organized, in both rural and urban areas.[28]

Indeed, one of the problems with contemporary Anglican ecclesiology as it is presented in the endless stream of reports and vision statements that Church House pumps out – from *Mission-Shaped Church* to *Vision and Strategy* – is that it has unmoored itself from the Church as embodied in the local church serving its community. It has internalized the idea that the secular writes the agenda to such an extent that the Church as an historical institution developed over centuries is sidelined in favour of a free-floating and fashion-conscious 'mission of the Holy Spirit' at work in the world, with the Church as a lacklustre follower, somewhat in the rear.

John Hull even criticized the *Mission-Shaped Church* report for being *too* church centred, and not realizing that the Kingdom of God is the aim of God's mission and the Church only one instrument.[29] He saw the relation with neighbour and the call to justice as the way to 'be church', in a mode of pure 'Anglican Bonhoefferism' that will be explored further in the next chapter.[30] For such a view, Christ is active within society in just and generous actions but this is seen as disenfranchising the Church, instead of recognizing the Church as the place where justice and generosity are made manifest, offered and fully realized. It is a basically over-individualized perspective, which abandons the Anglican legacy of understanding the Church as the truest *society*. Justice and generosity need habitual embedding and organizational support. They require stability and commitment over time, which the parish embodies.

Alongside this suppression of the Church as social in space goes an equal suppression of the reality of Church through time. There is an excessive presentism that must ironically undermine the present, which is only ever present as the gift of the past and the promise of the future. Both revelatory origins and eschatological expectation appear to have been forgotten. The two suppressions come together in Rowan Williams' surprisingly reductive definition (was it really his own?) offered when he was Archbishop of Canterbury: Church is 'what happens when people encounter the Risen Jesus and commit themselves to sustaining and deepening that encounter in their encounter with each other'.[31] In casting Church as an event merely subsequent to individuation, regarded as a process that develops in the future, there is little room for the creative role of tradition and the collective structure of belonging, which alone enables individual development. Language such as Williams's in this instance is repeated all over the missiology of contemporary Anglicanism. *Everyone* will make nice remarks about the value of the parochial model, but there is no genuine place for it in their vision.

Indeed, the mission to supposedly isolated individuals trumps everything in contemporary Anglican 'official' pronouncements and this means that, rather than being there as a witness to the glory of God, the Church and the people of God are subsumed as mere instruments of God's self-advertising campaign. But mission is simply a noun that needs to be supplied with some verbal content. The term is so overused that it makes one look back on the Decade of Evangelism with some nostalgia, since at least in those days the word 'evangelism' had the sense of the gospel (*evangelium*): the good news of the birth, death, and resurrection of Christ. If the great commissions at the end of the gospels of Matthew and John mean anything, it is to baptize, teach and feed, implying in John 21 both intellectual nourishment and the Eucharist in the phrase 'feed my lambs'. God's mission is the serene outpouring of life, love and knowledge and we best share in that mission by a positive desire to participate in it, rather than on account of a negatively panicked impulse, which informs so much of the 'mission-priority' language. If we are missionary disciples, as *Vision and Strategy*, the latest iteration of this missional project, calls us to be, then we *are* the good news we proclaim, in lives shaped by a knowledge, love and life in God in his Church. Our human medium is our message, and we are performing the continued arrival of the divine humanity, not marketing a God in retreat who is in need of a better publicity-machine.

Despite all this, the mission of the Church of England to the nation continues heroically in many places. As the then vicar of St James Rotherham with its East Dene estate, Abi Thompson wrote in 2017: 'Being the parish church gives you the incredible right to believe that everybody belongs here. People trust you with just about anything. It's understood that you are here for everybody who lives in your parish: everyone is a member.'[32] If people on a northern estate can still recognize the parish as theirs, and, indeed, that it grounds their trust in locality, the parish will have a future.

The new centralizing and parish merging initiatives, however, put this incarnational presence at risk. If carried through in many dioceses, they will make the national Anglican commitment to local embodiment impossible. And yet everything in our fractured, atomized society shows the opportunity for the Church to be a gathering and serving presence as never before. As Abi Thompson goes on to say: 'Has the parish had its day in Rotherham? Absolutely not – in fact, the need is greater than ever. Is it exhausting, demanding, all-consuming, and difficult? Yes; but Jesus never promised an easy life.'[33]

2

How Did We Get Here?

Man is ... essentially a story-telling animal. That means I can
only answer the question 'what am I to do?' if I can answer
the prior question of 'what story or stories do I find myself a
part of?'[1]

The stories we inhabit about the past are crucial in the way we
decide to act. The history of the parish outlined in the previous
chapter revealed much more commonality across different
Anglican traditions about the parish than might be imagined.
So how is it that we confront such fissures between different interpretations about the Church and her mission today?
Before launching into a critique of present policies, I want to try
to answer this question by reaching back into our more recent
past to discern where the theological roots of the present crisis
lie.

I am going to retrace the story that helps to explain where
we English Anglicans find ourselves today in the aftermath of
the Second World War. We cannot avoid statistics, but I shall
seek to suggest that theology and liturgy are equally important
drivers and that the story is not one of simple and inevitable
Christian decline. If I were to narrate that topic, I would have
to go back to the Enlightenment, in which religious claims were
not just put under scrutiny but denied their place at the philosophical high table. For Kant religion was a matter of merely
practical reason, and for the Enlightenment *philosophes* much
traditional religious practice was 'superstitious'. Despite the
challenge to Enlightenment rationalism by various shades of
post-modernism of the past fifty years, we still live under the
shadow of its unreconstructed ideology for which ancient ways

of life and practices are to be superseded on principle, because change is always presented as 'progress' and necessarily an improvement on what went before.

New ideas and methods are not necessarily better. I vividly recall having tea with an elderly academic couple in Cambridge who provided us with virulent neon-coloured slices of angel cake, which tasted of cardboard, announcing with great glee, how much cake had improved now the 'fuddy-duddy' days of baking your own were past. Little did they dream that the next century would unveil 'The Great British Bake-Off'.

The Anglican Church has been susceptible to a similar way of thinking, which equally risks being wrong-footed, so that the parish, as an ancient institution, is necessarily problematic, and is routinely described, almost always disparagingly, as 'inherited church', and thus something that ought to be consigned to the ecclesial attic, precisely because it is venerable – as if Church always newly descended from an ideal empyrean and had not been established in time by Christ, to be indeed inherited by us. As C. S. Lewis said, 'We all want progress. But progress means getting nearer to the place where you want to be. And if you have taken a wrong turning then to go forward does not get you any nearer.'[2] The turning away from all finite turnings of time and place, which are the only available ones, is the most fatal deviation of all. The Incarnation reveals to us that the givenness of our physicality and our mortality – our human limitations – are creative opportunities, hallowed by God himself.

We live today in a culture that promotes 'progress' as a virtue while at the same time denying the underlying teleology that would give one a sense of a goal for which to strive, because there can be none in a purely material account of reality. The same lack of *telos* or aim that would shape and drive our action is characteristic of Anglican policy documents. They are full of the language of mission to such an extent that it becomes wearisome, but the word 'mission' (*apostolē*), meaning a sending, appears but once in the New Testament, in Galatians 2.8. That is presumably because people are only sent for a specific identifiable purpose: to preach the gospel, to witness, reconcile, and baptize. When one looks for the aim of *Vision and Strategy*,

the most recent strategy document promulgated by the archbishops, one reads this:

> The overriding aim for the future is that any worshipping
> member of the Church of England, when asked by their friend
> where they could go to explore their faith, would be able to
> recommend an expression of Church locally that would really
> suit them.[3]

The only aim here is that of personal choice, as if selecting a
brand of cereal in a supermarket. But with the trajectory away
from parish ministry and the threat of mergers and closures,
the *smorgasbord* of 'choice' will not include the parish church
among its possibilities. As so often, the prioritizing of choice
is itself covertly selective; the promotion of 'choice' in food-
outlets, for example, tends to ensure that the market renders
your local pub, reachable by foot, no longer viable.

There are three priorities given below these words, which are
more substantive: 'to become a church of missionary disciples
… to be a church where mixed ecology is the norm … to be a
church that is younger and more diverse', but even these are
proximate goals and put the focus on altering the nature and
constituency of the Church rather than on an evidence-based
delivery plan for converting the young, empowering and
enriching the formation of believers, and so forth. Bizarrely, for
policies in flight from traditional ecclesiology, instead of taking
the institution for granted and working out from it creatively,
the language is all about 'church' as such. And it is all too clear
that the assumption behind the words of *Vision and Strategy*
is an unexamined notion that the parish church may not 'suit'
many people. This is the secular language of consumer choice.
It is a curious 'marketing strategy' that goes headlong in quest
of the categories of people that evidence suggests are least likely
to be its customers, while expecting to keep the existing takers
for the product. Many retail chains have foundered thus.

Since the whole point of the parish system is that it is for
everyone, offering a liturgical round suited to the real needs of
all, whether they know this or not, this undermines faith in the

very DNA of Anglicanism and its liturgies. There have always been chaplaincies, of course, but they too instantiate parochial values, being quasi-parishes for a defined group who are often necessarily distinct from ordinary life, such as the armed forces or the prison service. By contrast, the language used by the archbishop is that of elective individualism: 'explore their faith' and 'suit them'. It is not confident about promoting the Christian gospel but suggests it as merely one possible mode of self-development. Vanished from this attitude is any sense that Christianity is already fitted universally to the deepest spiritual needs of all.

So where did this apologetic attitude to the parish and faith generally come from? I believe it is an outworking of particular theological trends in the 1960s and beyond, although its roots do go back to the Enlightenment and the rise of historical criticism in the nineteenth century.

It is important to emphasize that the story of the Church in the twentieth century is not one of simple continued decline. In the aftermath of the Second World War, for example, the Church of England saw some striking growth and seemed to be in touch with the popular mood. This was a period of continued rationing and hardship, but of great hope in a new Elizabethan Age: it saw the arrival of the Welfare State, which was rather like the secular arm of the Church as a universal provider in which we all had a stake, and all had rights. It was a future Archbishop of Canterbury, William Temple, who was the first to use the term in print, long before his elevation, in a work of 1928, in which he opposed welfare-state to power-state as one that served the flourishing of all its citizens.[4] The Butler Education Act of 1944 and the National Health Service owe a considerable amount to Temple and his friends R. H. Tawney and William Beveridge, with the latter's report published in the same year as the Malvern Conference, which Temple chaired.

Much of what church leaders discussed at Malvern in 1941, as they sought a complete social and economic reconstruction after the war was over, chimed with the project of the 1945 Attlee government, especially in the fields of education, housing and social security. The post-war settlement, with higher taxation and death duties for the wealthy, the welfare state and nationalization of some industries, made it seem as if the radical Christianizing of the nation, with its roots in Victorian Anglican theology, was well under way. And while all this was the fruit of a Labour government and the Church of England was still a predominantly Conservative institution, we forget how much consensus there was between parties prior to the Thatcher revolution on the welfare state and even on economic matters. As Churchill said in 1952: 'Four-fifths of both parties agree on four-fifths of what should be done, and after all, we all sink or swim together on our perilous voyage ever-accelerating into the unknown.'[5] The very fact that Church leaders were planning reconstruction during the horrors of war showed they had confidence in their mission to the nation and that they had something to contribute.

We need a similar national programme of spiritual and moral reconstruction in the present crisis, but our leaders show little appetite or ambition for such an event as the Malvern Conference, where the Church invited the top intellectuals in its ranks as well as radical practitioners to confer. Malvern had its limits, but as an idea it was wholly admirable and it meant that when the war ended, the Church had already thought ahead to the needs of a war-weary people.

As I write, our country is dealing with crumbling institutions and an economic downturn, with the climate emergency ever more pressing. One thing is clear: it is expected that the crisis will only deepen. How is the Common Good to be discerned amid all this? Instead of a holistic intellectual analysis of our spiritual path ahead we have two main responses. One is the constant drip of social media interventions by senior clergy, feeling they need to respond to every news item as if they were secular politicians; the other is target-led demands on often economically stricken parishes to become carbon-neutral by 2030, a date brought forward during a general synod debate without sufficient funds and preparations having been clearly established in advance to make this realistically achievable. Without that initial theological discussion, there is no sense of direction in all this, and the tweeting can too easily take a party-political edge and be discounted. Bishops and archbishops should speak rarely, but with authority garnered from proper theological analysis and deep thought. Then such pronouncements would be taken more seriously. The constant positioning makes it hard to discern the Common Good driver in what they say.

One way in which a more confident Church communicated in the mid-twentieth century was through lay experts on radio programmes. The advent of radio indeed increased the prominence of Anglican Christianity in British culture in the mid-twentieth century with the likes of T. S. Eliot, Dorothy Sayers and C. S. Lewis all broadcasting regularly during the wartime years and beyond. Religion was allowed eight hours per week, which included everything from services to Sayers' plays on the life of Christ, *The Man Born to be King,* which aired in 1941.[6] Religious programmes also had large followings. A study of greater Derby in 1954 found that 56% of the adult population listened to religious programmes, of whom only one in eight had been to church the previous Sunday.[7]

It is in that idealistic context that the Church of England as a national institution, locally grounded, achieved some significant post-war growth. A Gallup poll of 1946 saw 83% of the population identifying with one of the mainline churches, *rising* to 90% in 1963. In the late forties, just under half the population never attended church while in 1963 *three quarters* claimed to attend occasionally.[8] The Church of England enjoyed the lion's share of affiliation, as well as baptisms, weddings and so on.

This is very much the Church of England in which I grew up, with a full provision of social activities, busy Sunday School and robed choir in many churches, including the mainly council-housing parish of St Luke's Portsea, where I first attended church. This was the era of socially concerned parish priests like Bill Sargent of St Mark's Portsea who started a Housing Association and led colourful processions through the busy streets. Curates at St Mary Portsea regularly broke up fights outside their house on a Friday night. While certainly no idyll, working-class Portsea was an area that witnessed lively and engaged ministry in the inner city, well respected and confident. This assuredness was a wider phenomenon and nationally, the numbers of worshippers would be maintained above two million until 1970.

As Andrew Brown and Linda Woodhead point out in their insightful, if trenchant, analysis of 'How the Church of England Lost the English People', 'the success of the Church for so many centuries has lain in its ability to remain articulated with English society, not just by running alongside it like a page before a stagecoach, but by helping it to sustain and understand itself'.[9] The society I grew up in was one that was relatively secure in its new post-war unity and focused on a common good. At my senior school, the motto was from Joshua: 'be ye strong and very courageous', and we were encouraged to fulfil these words by our integrity and service. We were urged (as girls, be it noted) to choose professions that would serve society and this vocational ethic flowed from Christian values.

Such traditionalism nonetheless coincided with a period when the gap between rich and poor was closing, thanks in part to an efficiently functioning welfare state and a higher school-leaving age. We all sang the 'Song of Liberty' to Elgar's *Pomp and Circumstance* 4 at my state junior school and 'When a knight won his spurs' in assembly. Church, school and society appeared to share common values and our lives were experienced as remarkably integrated by today's standards.

The Church has witnessed an enormous loss of numbers since the times that I am describing, and has lost the will, the authority and the ability to perform this integrating role. The reasons for the decline are hotly contested by sociologists. Callum Brown, who questionably tends to cast the 1950s as a period of repression and conformity, emphasizes the revolt of housewives in the 1960s as they took on more paid work – ignoring the overwhelmingly capitalist imperatives that were newly requiring them to do so and the overriding preference of working-class women to stay at home. Other scholars note increased mobility and the ability to go on trips on Sunday, as well as the advent of television: one recalls how the *Forsyte Saga* destroyed Sunday evening worship. The sexual revolution had its part to play, alongside the general turning away from traditional modes of life and behaviour, as well as the growing lack of respect for older people and institutions, as the 'heroic generation' became increasingly the object of ungrateful satire. In a culmination of this cultural liberalism (now increasingly under revisionist scrutiny by historians), a succeeding economic liberalism finally permitted shops to open on Sunday in the 1990s. This changed the character of that day immeasurably and altered the entire character of the British weekend overnight: the familial and the sacral was increasingly swamped by the commercial and its accompanying solitude.

David Martin questions the universality and inevitability of the secularization narrative, which looks rather different (at least up till now) from a global perspective. Moreover, Tom Holland in *Dominion* concludes that secularism is itself indebted to Christianity. Without it, 'no one would have ever got woke'.[10] Yet all agree that from the 1960s onwards we entered a period of more global and free-wheeling capitalism, in which the individual trumps the relational, and consumer choices define people's identities.

The question that concerns us here is how the Church of England responded to this undoubted enormous challenge. Are Brown and Woodhead correct in arguing that it is the Church that is responsible for losing the English people? Have we colluded in our own marginalization? To a degree of course, an answer 'yes' to these questions would confirm Martin's questioning of the secularization process as absolutely inevitable.

Bonhoeffer and Religionless Christianity

While I nonetheless do not think for a moment that the Church could have altogether stopped the juggernaut that is secularization as an overwhelming tendency, I do believe that we have deliberately made our situation harder for ourselves by internalizing secular attitudes. One could of course argue that that, in itself, is witness to the force of the secularizing process, and yet if one denies its absolute inevitability, then we must pay more attention to the contingency of this internalization.

One very considerable factor here is the influence of the heroic German Lutheran theologian Dietrich Bonhoeffer, who was executed by the Nazis in 1945 for his part in a plot to assassinate Hitler. His great friend Eberhard Bethge carefully preserved the letters he wrote from Tegen prison and later published them, with the first English translation appearing in 1953.

The letters are personal and highly speculative, as they begin to imagine how to live a life of faith in a post-war world. Bonhoeffer takes his Lutheran theology of the cross to such a dialectical extreme that he envisages what he calls 'religionless Christianity', in which we share Christ's suffering by plunging into a godless world without any veneer of religion.[11] Whether Bonhoeffer would have changed or clarified his words had he lived, we shall never know. His martyrdom, as it came to be interpreted, gave his 'last will and testament', as SCM Press described it in a recent blurb, immense authority.

In his interesting study of what he calls 'English Bonhoeffer-ism', Mark Chapman names John Robinson as just one of those captivated by the *Letters*, but he was surely the most influential, rendering Bonhoeffer a prophetic voice in *Honest to God* in 1963.[12] Bonhoeffer was deployed to justify a turn away from care for the 'religious' and towards a ministry defined by the secular. This was the practice in the Diocese of Southwark at the time, with Nicholas Stacey's radical social initiatives and his eventual withdrawal into social work. God was now supposed to be not present in the churches, whose deity was the traditional 'out there', transcendent divinity, and 'the churches were not worth keeping, at least in their present form'.[13] Christ was already immanent in the secular world at a satisfactory end of history, and all the Church had to do was 'to give voice to this latent Christian tendency present in all people'.[14] What the people needed to be saved from was no longer sin but the supposed staleness of religious language, customs and liturgy.

I have listened to sermons on Bonhoeffer countless times because soon the *Letters* and *The Cost of Discipleship* became standard texts in theological training. To question Bonhoeffer was viewed by the retired clergy officiating at Southwell Minster as a form of heresy, because for their generation, he was the saint and prophet of the century. This view crosses the divide between different Anglican parties. There is a beautiful poem by the high Anglican Geoffrey Hill, 'Christmas Trees', about Bonhoeffer's prison writings, and in 2018 students at the evangelical Trinity College Bristol were studying these same texts and finding Bonhoeffer 'an inspired theologian'.[15] It is a phrase from Bonhoeffer that gives the 'new monasticism' its title, although the various contemporary modes (apart from the St Anselm's Community at Lambeth) are quite gentle and 'light' in the demands made of adherents compared to the poverty and rigour of Bonhoeffer's conception, or of the practice of Finkenwalde, his alternative seminary.

There is much to admire in Bonhoeffer, especially in his earlier and complex theology, with its acute existential as well as metaphysical awareness, but I would argue that the uncritical reception of his 'religionless Christianity', usually taken out of its context of the confessing church under Nazism, has been pernicious, and has meant that for fifty years and more there has been a theological warrant for regarding the worshipping congregation as somehow lacking, and traditional forms as ambiguous. I heard a bishop at a conference recently refer to the 'rump of believers' and I am sure that Bonhoeffer lurks somewhere behind such a view. John Robinson's *Honest to God* has the following quotation from Bonhoeffer about those people who are still open to the need for religion:

> The only people left for us to light on in the way of 'religion' are a few 'last survivals of the age of chivalry', or else one or two, who are intellectually dishonest. Would they be the chosen few? Is it on this dubious group and none other that we are to pounce, in fervour, pique or indignation, in order to sell them the goods that we have to offer? Are we to fall upon one or two unhappy people in their weakest moments and force upon them a sort of religious coercion?[16]

This, he argues, is where the contemporary Church operates.

While one can sympathize with the desire not to exploit the vulnerable, there is very little confidence in the value of the current congregation here, who often include as many who are staunchly or imaginatively heroic, as are weak or resentful. Yet those who need or value religion were already regarded as 'a dubious group' or as 'intellectually dishonest' by Bonhoeffer himself. You can still see this language used today, as in Barry Hill's 2021 *Church Times* comment piece, which claimed that 'for decades, the primacy of the congregation has been one of the C of E's most pervasive institutional sins, from which many other sins concerning power, control, and defensiveness flow'.[17] He believes that caring for the congregation has downgraded outreach to the whole community and that other modes of Fresh Expression are needed to reach them, although he gives no reason why this should be so, except that 'church culture' is problematic. This seems to mean liturgy.

What goes along with this denigration of the existing congregation is a theology, curiously not altogether unlike that of F. D. Maurice, which views the non-religious as latently Christian. Maurice believed that the sacraments of baptism revealed the true identity of the person as child of God, rather than effecting a new identity by adoption. Yet in contrast to Maurice, who wanted everyone included in the Church, with baptism operating as a kind of Platonic recollection of transcendence, too often in the liberal and liberal-catholic wings of the Church of England today this can be employed to affirm and confirm non-believers in their secular self-sufficiency. Again, I have listened to several sermons where the non-religious are held to be on their own spiritual quest, the direction and value of which is inherently authentic, and therefore they should not be interfered with; nor do they need the gospel preached to them. As in John Robinson's anthropological vision, they have 'come of age' and are beyond the nursery leading-strings of religion.[18] Religion, for Robinson, following Bonhoeffer in a notably less anguished and mystically dialectical mode, was an idol, and needed to be replaced by the authentic living of an existentialist creed, which he derived from Paul Tillich.

In consequence, this all-too-English Bonhoefferism, jettisoning an older and profounder English Christian Platonism, justifies ignoring those already in the pews while merely smiling beneficently on those outside. It leads to an ambiguous attitude to the faith, in which one apologizes for it and for imposing it on others. Mark Chapman quotes Valerie Pitt, who had been associated with the South Bank theologians and their journal, *Prism*, but who fell out of love with its 'religionless' vision and denigration of parochial life. She asks, 'it is worth enquiring whether the withdrawal of our talents, of our love from all the disturbing, irritating, misguided pew fodder isn't one of the reasons why it's so provincial, so closed in a sub-Christian world'.[19] And she suggests that the way forward is to initially withdraw into it, even though, she notes sardonically, 'for a while it will be dreadfully provincial – like the Lord's life in Galilee'.[20]

Chapman has sympathy for Pitt's position because, unlike Brown and Woodhead, he does not think that the problem is that the Church has abandoned her national task of reflection of the currently dominant English identity. For him, 'religionless Christianity' was a last-ditch attempt to do *just that* and to render the whole country, even in its self-enclosed secularity, as obscurely holy. His view is in synergy with the bold thesis of Sam Brewitt-Taylor, who claims in *Christian Radicalism and the British Sixties* that Robinson and his South Bank friends invented a particularly British theological form of secularity, embracing politics, egalitarianism and liberal sexuality, which they then made available for other players. [21]

Most significantly for my argument, Brewitt-Taylor believes that it was Christians who were the *first* to claim that the modern age was, indeed, secular, following the Bonhoeffer terminology, and that these radical Christians are partly the *authors* of changes in perception of the relevance of the Church, rather than reflecting something that had already spontaneously arisen. He suggests that it is no coincidence that 'the years between 1961 and 1964, which saw the sudden elite and perhaps predominantly *Christian* elite reinvention of modernity as 'secular', also saw 'the beginnings of the catastrophic falls in the ecclesiastical statistics from which the mainstream Protestant churches have never recovered', citing evidence that clergy themselves were conveying this modish but dubiously grounded language to their communities.[22]

The effect on clergy morale of the language of secularization was significant, Brewitt-Taylor argues, and the whole *Honest to God* debate was destabilizing. Robinson's supporters, David Edwards opined at the time, 'are ready to declare themselves in favour of change even when they do not see exactly where the process of change will end' and Brewitt-Taylor points out that the result of this view was that any ideas perceived as traditional were subverted and the new legitimated, however vague and various it might be.[23]

In consequence, the problem remains to this day that to defend the parochial system as I seek to do is to be wrong-footed from the start, since the traditional has lost any claim to worth. This is true in our culture as a whole across different sites and disciplines. No longer are schoolchildren being taught the foundational literary texts; they learn little history before World War I and what they do learn is presented in a progressivist mode; ideas of learning a craft or the ethics of a profession are equally set aside, all because they are regarded as antiquated.[24] And yet, what Brewitt-Wood's book demonstrates is that secularizations are contingent, not teleological, however they may become entrenched and habituated. They are ultimately, from the Enlightenment onwards, constructed narratives, which only gradually confirm themselves through their rhetorical and then lived-out excess. A Whig suspicion of the religious past as holding back secular progress as though it were an eternal residual norm can be trumped by a *much more critical* post-modern exposure of secularization as the triumph of quests for cognitive power and control, as the maverick Peterhouse historian Maurice Cowling showed in conspicuous detail in the case of modern England since the nineteenth century.[25]

Thus, our speeded-up secularization in the 1960s was demonstrably in part the Church's own theological creation, embodying a realized eschatological vision in which the Kingdom of God was already secretly manifest in secular culture. A rather different British Hegelianism from the one that had helped develop older public glories through positive beneficent action was now in effect to the fore. Nothing after all need any longer be done: history had on its own already completed a satisfactory negative work, leaving the citizen in the bliss of material contentment and freedom of choice. A bit of emancipatory and egalitarian tidying-up was all that remained to be performed and this was now held to be the authentic work of the Gospel.

Yet Brown and Woodhead blame the Church for departing from its public role only in the Thatcher years, when Archbishop Runcie commissioned the *Faith in the City* report, and increasingly the Church became oppositional in its relation to society. I would argue to the contrary that this opposition derived from a residual reassertion of the pre-1960s communitarian vision. For good or ill, Margaret Thatcher's political project gave up on the consensual post-war settlement, now economically as well as culturally; it was inherently controversial, separating people along ideological fault-lines. There was, therefore, no way that the Church could avoid conflict in seeking to address a divided Britain.

Nonetheless, Thatcher's opponents had also diluted the older consensus. *Faith in the City* reported in the manner of a Royal Commission; and the number of recommendations aimed at the state – twenty-three – as opposed to the thirty-eight to the Church – meant that the report focused on specific policy proposals. Yet, however worthy these recommendations might have been, they were divorced from a substantive Christian social vision as had been offered in the past, whether in the corporatist social democratic version of Temple or the rather less statist and more plurally corporatist vision of V. C. Demant and the Christendom Group (of which T. S. Eliot had been the most famous member). The theological element was just not front and foremost, and when theology *was* introduced in Anthony Harvey's contribution, it was from Latin American Liberation Theology rather than Anglicanism's own substantial body of social theology.[26]

Much good came out of the report in terms of money for and attention to deprived urban parishes, but the idea of local theologies promulgated by Harvey and developed further in his edited collection, *Theology in the City: A Theological Response to 'Faith in the City,* did not so much encourage reflection on a *common* Christian theology in a particular place and situation as suggest the inviolability of multiple, personally conceived theologies. Andrew Hake's contribution, moreover, contained a strong 'religionless' element: one could develop a Christian formation without any relation to the Church and the language used in urban liturgy need not be overtly theological: only 'implicitly'.[27]

The consensus of the 1950s had worked because the Church's theology chimed with the national self-understanding but was confidently theological. The 'Parish and People' movement of that era, which successfully made the Eucharist the central liturgy in most Anglican churches, arose from the heart of high-church or 'liberal Catholic' Anglican theology, which was to the fore in the mid-century and united it with the participatory egalitarianism of the 'soft' side of South Bank theology. By contrast, the viewpoint of *Faith in the City* did not emerge from this long and complex legacy at all. Ironically, its Royal Commission mode represented a high point of establishment influence and yet the secular tone of its content foretold a swallowing by the more left-liberal wing of that establishment. If nothing like this document has been attempted since, then arguably that is because this document itself rendered that unlikely.

Biblical Criticism and the Dearth of Theology in Theological Education

The study of the Christian scriptures as any other book was also predominantly a fruit of the Enlightenment. It was, again, primarily German historical scholarship that led to the schools of form, redaction, reader-response theory and so on. It has limitations, in that in its purest, most sceptical form, for example, it takes a dark view of any apparently 'high' Christological claims for Jesus in the New Testament, and attributes them to later early church intervention. For some scholars, anything that suits a Christian worldview is to be discounted as authentically historical, begging the questions of why we have a New Testament at all, and why we should assume that only the 'disenchanted' is real – an issue upon which historiography is after all not qualified to decide.

Today there exist whole swathes of biblical scholarship that are far more generous and theological in character and some of the positivist scepticism is very much a thing of the past. In current biblical scholarship there is the figure of N. T. Wright, not to mention John Barclay, Walter Moberley, Stephen Fowl, Walter Brueggemann, Ellen Davis, Catharine Dell, Richard Hays, David Bentley Hart and many others who approach the Bible with respect and theological depth. Meanwhile, several philosophers like Alain Badiou, Giorgio Agamben and David Lloyd Dusenbury have recognized that the New Testament presents sophisticated theoretical and political ideas in a symbolic and narrative fashion: they are returning the reading of the Bible to the mainstream of western culture.

While American conservative Protestantism has embraced some of the above more doctrinal biblical approaches, many older British clergy were educated in the most sceptical Bultmann tradition, for which much is attributed to 'myth' and a sharp distinction is drawn between the mythological-religious on the one hand, and the scientific or historical on the other. As a student, having previously studied English and classical literatures, I was never convinced by the positivistic method; it seemed an inappropriate way to address any text whatsoever. Ironically, my first supervisor at Cambridge in New Testament was that same John Robinson of *Honest to God* and he seemed curiously to be as conservative as I in relation to New Testament study and was even at the time claiming John's Gospel to be the earliest. Yet generations of clergy have been brought up on Bultmann and his hermeneutics (however qualified) and make a sharp distinction between that study and the bland pietism that they so often offer to their congregations, who are in effect not quite let into the modern gnostic secret of sceptical critique. Alternately, they do preach in this liberal mode for which the Bible only matters when we agree with it.

Just as destabilizing is the Christian Union way of dealing with biblical criticism at university. Those of a more fundamentalist cast tend to treat such study as a kind of diabolical ordeal, so that they have recourse to a special Christian Union group that supports theology students and gets them through it. That is not satisfactory either, especially since fundamentalism is itself a post-Enlightenment theory of inspiration as positivistically literal, and such withdrawal prevents real intellectual engagement. Some clergy nourished in this tradition lack the confidence to treat the Bible theologically, and this is to the disservice of the Church and particularly their congregations.

The outworkings of these two tendencies lead to particularly unhelpful ways of reading the Old Testament. The Bultmannesque liberal is particularly to the fore in describing it as some great horror-chamber of a punitive God zapping everyone until the peace-loving Christ of the New Testament came along. You either get a crude supercessionism on the liberal side, or an evangelical tendency to think that the main characters of the Hebrew Bible are there to emulate as heroes, when often they are being deeply ironized by the narrative as flawed and misguided.

Part of the reason why today our important conversations about gender and sexuality are so toxic is that we lack a theological account of Scripture by which to understand the biblical material. Even *Living in Love and Faith*, the materials given to use to open such conversations, tended to focus on single verses as proof texts, if only proof texts about the need to be kind and inclusive. So where are our hermeneutical principles? How do we read hard texts with charity? How does tradition play a part? I fear that in the end we will make epoch-making decisions on these matters with no other values apart from being nice or the proffering of texts torn from their contexts and wielded like weapons for which there could be no reasonable defence.

Part of our problem is that, apart from the highly assured ranks of Holy Trinity Brompton and conservative evangelicals, we lack a confidence in our scriptures, our theology and tradition. In former days clergy were formed by their college-based ordination training in which theological study was integrated into a regular life of communal worship and private prayer. Far fewer ordinands enjoy residential training these days and even those who do find the curriculum shrinking in terms of Christian doctrine, history and liturgy. The era of *Honest to God* is long gone and the non-realist theology of the Sea of Faith Network is very much a minority sport. And yet theology is not given its proper place at the heart of the Church, and we are so much the poorer for it. Indeed, it is like trying to steer a steamer without an engine.

Liturgical Experimentation

Until recently, the Church of England had one Book of Common Prayer, which united in one form of worship the disparate wings of the Church. Following the experience of chaplains in World War I and the rise of a more general catholicity of practice in most parts of the Church, the Anglican Church sought modest revisions of its Prayer Book, which were passed easily in Convocations of the clergy but failed to pass in Parliament. The main change in the Eucharist was the inclusion of a proper calling down of the Holy Spirit upon the gifts, an *epiclesis,* to accord both with early church practice and a richer understanding of the action of God in the rite. Had 1928 been made fully official, it is possible that we might have revised it again more organically and kept the sense of one prayer book for all Anglicans. This is important, since it is because the Church of England has no overall authority in the way the Roman Catholic Church does, that the *lex orandi lex credendi* idea matters so much. The law of our prayer is the law of what we believe. Changing the liturgy then alters our whole way of believing. We have gained some substantive and thoughtful liturgies in the many waves of revision that have passed over us and rich provision for the liturgical cycle and for the agricultural year. Unfortunately, however, the revisions have come at a low time for the English language, which has lost the earthy directness and poetic plangency of Cranmer's English and is flatter and more abstract. People brought up as children with the BCP can recite whole chunks of it because its language is made for such memorizing, and it will be a resource to them all their lives.

Moreover, we have lost the sense of unity that the single rite gave us. I can recall attending the Cambridge Christian Union Mattins at the Round Church in Cambridge, which was identical to the rite at St Botolph's, St Bene't's or any other Anglican Church one might care to name. Many people carried their prayer book to church on Sunday and it had everything they needed: there was no need for weekly sheets or the dreaded screen, since many copies had the hymn book in the back. Much evidence would suggest that this literally bound liturgical unity retains much appeal and not least amongst the more critically reflective young people. The vicar of Brenchley, Campbell Paget, reports that at his strongly flourishing parish church, it is the elderly who are attracted to café church, while younger people prefer traditional liturgy.

Changing liturgical order or form for theological reasons is one thing, but the Church has also sought to make the liturgies more relevant and understandable by ordinary people. This sounds like a worthy project, but it is doomed. There is no way in the end that you can reduce worship down to a wholly comprehensible level. Salvation, redemption, resurrection, sin, incarnation are words that are hard to do without or to paraphrase. The Alternative Baptism texts, endeavouring to avoid theological language, substitute 'turn away' from sin, saying blandly 'We all wander from God and lose our way', which substitutes a journey metaphor for that of new life and the defeat of evil and loses any of the sense of drama and exorcism of the original rite.[28]

Only this week, I took a baptism service for a toddler and led a Christingle service for a congregation made up of young families. At both services the modern Lord's Prayer was the one printed, and on each occasion, the parents stumbled over the words, still trying to say the traditional form. Not only had the Church modernized for no appreciable benefit in terms of accessibility – for the new version of the prayer still includes 'lead us not into temptation', which is hardly modern English – but we continually disenfranchise those who learnt the prayer as children but are not recent attenders. It would be unthinkable in any other religious tradition, such as Islam, to abandon a traditional central prayer's wording in this way.

This chapter has argued that although the Church of England faces the challenges of secularism and shares a steep decline in membership with trade unions, political parties, and civic associations of all kinds, it has nonetheless lost confidence in itself for quite other reasons. The seed of the present lack of interest in worshipping congregations can be traced back to Bonhoeffer's 'religionless' Christianity and *Honest to God*, while the dearth of theology at a deep level has affected our confidence and ability to respond to the depth of the challenges we face.

The honourable exception here is the Holy Trinity Brompton mode of pietism, which might not be highly theological, but which is relaxed and comfortable in its faith and its expression. To watch an HTB online Sunday service, with its couple in deckchairs offering a friendly introduction, and its clarity in conveying its message in the sermon, is instructive for all those who do not share its theology. There is a sense of hospitality, of calling people in to something that is intrinsically valuable that could be emulated by those who do not necessarily share HTB's belief in substitutionary atonement.

The nearest I have come to seeing such emulation is in a village context in the Yorkshire Dales, where the relaxed and generous parochial welcome came from the positive nature of the life of the community. They might have been conveying a gentle, inclusive, middle-of-the-road Anglicanism, but they did so with brio and enthusiasm, and trust in their own tradition. For in all the crises that face us we need to lose the sense of panic. Even if you are not undergirded with the millions of HTB and are not sure where the money to mend the roof is coming from, Christ's gospel cannot fail. Later in this book I shall seek to argue that the parish system also need not fail because it has practical strengths and an embodied theology that our culture desperately needs. But first and foremost, we need to have confidence in the Church of England, her liturgies and traditions as well as in the divine mystery that worship should evoke.

3

Following the Money

'For where your treasure is, there will your heart be also', says Christ in Matthew 6.21. One of the clearest ways in which the Church of England demonstrates her sense of priorities is how she spends her money and allocates her resources. This chapter will examine the way parish clergy numbers have been reduced and clerical freedom with it, how resources have been taken away from parishes and where money is now squandered on so-called mission projects. It will draw attention to the way parishes are merged and how plans are afoot to make it easier to close and sell churches. Overall, we shall see a picture of dereliction of the responsibility to be a Christian presence in every community and a shocking betrayal of trust.

The Clergy

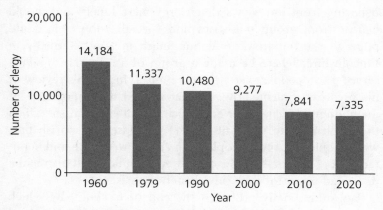

Figure 2: Total FTE Clergy in the Church of England.
Source: Church of England Statistics.

Numbers of clergy have steadily shrunk. In 1959, for example, there were still 13,075 stipendiary parish clergy, whereas in 2020 there were only just over 7,000. Despite this, the numbers of senior clergy remain more or less the same, while the number of archdeacons rose from 106 to 129.[1] Seeing that the creation of new archdeacon posts comes on apace, that number will by now have swollen further, with a new post of associate archdeacon to add to the mix, of which Oxford diocese alone has three associates, along with its four archdeacons, as well as an array of administrative support that academics can only dream of.[2]

From these figures, you can see how the senior levels of command remain stable over time or increase, even while they have fewer clergy to look after and smaller congregations (down from 1,541,821 in 1970 to 679,800 in 2019), while front-line clergy numbers are reduced, and much use is made of retired clergy and Self-Supporting Ministers.

This reduction in clergy numbers goes even further back than the 1950s, of course, but it was in the 1960s and 70s that the centralization moves began. Leslie Paul's report of 1963–64, *The Deployment and Payment of the Clergy*, was the work of a sociologist, and sought to rationalize the provision of clergy across the land by numbers of population, rather than communities. He also wanted to organize clergy into teams, believing from interviews that clergy were lonely and would benefit from group ministries and specialization.[3] He could point to the initiative of Arthur Smith in South Ormsby in Lincolnshire, where he made a group of 12 churches, which served 1100 people over 75 square miles. In Smith's review of his own experiment, however, he stressed the importance of maintaining the character and specificity of each parish, which they were able to maintain by the purchase of a parish bus, which could transport people from church to church and maintain a core of worship in each and every building. It also had a dedicated priest for each tiny cluster of parishes.[4]

Paul additionally proposed the end of freehold, by which an incumbent of a benefice had ownership of it, its glebe land (and originally its tithe income), parsonage and fees until it was passed onto his successor. He wanted it adapted to a kind of leasehold, so that clergy could be organized more rationally in a model that was primarily utilitarian, and which showed little sympathy for rural ministry – despite the fact that the country-side was and remains today the heartland of Anglican practice, with less decline per capita than urban areas.

Clergy, in particular, were alarmed. Tindal Hart compared the nature of the cuts proposed to those of the railway 'bluebell lines', which removed trains that served a vital function, and he saw the proposals as signalling the inexorable though illogical withdrawal of the Church of England from its countryside heart, to become an urban sect.[5] Eric Treacy similarly detected the radicalism of the proposals, arguing 'that anything we do which has the effect of cutting at the roots will only become evident in a period of about fifty years'.[6] Sociologist Margaret Hewitt critiqued the report on social science grounds, showing that it ignored the historical dimension, especially in relation to freehold, which Paul wanted to be ended for reasons of expedi-ency even though 'historians have always held [it] to enshrine certain spiritual values'.[7] Freehold was a 'social prize in an increasingly authoritarian society'.[8] Bishop Barry of Southwell was prepared to see some modification of the freehold, but he lamented what he saw would be the outcome of the proposals: 'an increase in a bureaucracy run by ecclesiastical civil servants (with salaries far higher than those of the clergy) of which there is probably too much already'.[9] The fears of all these responders to the Paul report have been realized, with the huge increases in the size of diocesan administration and eyewatering salaries paid to some diocesan employees, such as the £90,000 adver-tised for the Archbishop of York's chief of staff, and the loss of freehold and independence from the clergy. All too many clergy do not have the status even of incumbent, but merely priest-in-charge, which makes them beholden to the archdeacon.

From these critical responses to the Paul Report, one can see how the roots of our present situation are deep and stretch far back into that same 1960s that saw the onset of 'religion-less Christianity' and the effects of *Honest to God*. Choosing a sociologist to write an independent report on how clergy should work was itself a secularizing move, and one that naturally produced proposals driven by sociological and managerial principles, with goals such as efficiency overriding defining spiritual purposes. The tendency to increase diocesan administrative posts was bound to accompany these principles, as they require someone to monitor how well such principles are being applied.

The principle of centralizing parishes into groups is very old now and has been enacted throughout the countryside. It was not, for the most part, organized through teams, which did not prove generally popular, because both clergy and laity preferred the priest and parish model. Instead, a cleric works frequently single-handed with a non-stipendiary colleague or a reader to assist. When the numbers were small, so that the priest could take a proper part in the life of each community, it worked well enough. I recall my own placement in the Three Tons group, with churches clustering near the Trent and an annual pilgrimage perambulating around all three. Even then the vicar had a key lay reader or children's worker in each church, so that evensong was sung, for example, regularly in the village of Upton, even in the incumbent's absence. Gradually, however, the groups have become completely unmanageable, until we are now reaching a point where whole swathes of country parishes are left in interregnum for as long as seven years or organized into ever larger groups, where the cure of souls necessarily means very little.

All the research shows that there is a link between cutting clergy and decline. *Going Deeper: Church Attendance Statistics and Clergy Deployment*, a study by the Revd Dr Fiona Tweedie, found that 'an increase in the number of clergy over time is associated with a greater likelihood of there being attendance growth. A decrease in clergy is associated with the greater likelihood of there being a decline in attendance growth.'[10] Another report, *From Anecdote to Evidence*, is even more emphatic:

The findings show that single church units under one leader are more likely to grow than when churches are grouped together. Analysing data across a range of congregation size categories shows that amalgamations of churches are more likely to decline. Moreover, the larger the number of churches in the amalgamation the more likely they are to decline. This is exacerbated when amalgamations have more churches.[11]

It is instructive that the example of growth in a small rural church in the report occurs when the curate in a multi-parish benefice institutes a weekly service with children's provision and visits everyone in the village, acting exactly like a single priest in a single parish, which is the model that most promotes increase![12] And it is not just Church of England research that makes this case. The Growing Churches Forums in the Baptist Union demonstrated that growth best happened when supported by clergy, even when a church is small. They also discovered that a church with a large fringe of people who might attend social events, rather than services, was also a driver – this being very much part of the parochial model.

Mergers and Amalgamations

So, from the beginning, attempts to amalgamate parishes in benefices were in reality instituting their decline, and the present plans, despite their constant genuflections to the parish ideal, will only destroy them. In Leicester Diocese, for example, 24 parishes with 35 churches are to be made into the Launde Minster Mission Community, with an oversight minister and an administrator. They intend to cut clergy numbers by 20 by 2026.[13] At the same time, they hope to have comparable numbers of new worshipping communities as parishes and claim that even if they did not have financial need as a driver, they would have made these changes in any case.[14] A remarkable admission of the priority of ideology and not exigency.

How eucharistic life is to be maintained along with any sense of the local church is in these circumstances impossible to envisage. Moreover, until Angela Tilby in her *Church Times* column pointed out that the appointment of a lay person as oversight minister gave them the cure of souls, and went against Anglican orders, that was an option in each minster area. The vicar would have been a layman or woman, not a priest. This was quickly withdrawn the day of the vote in the diocesan synod, thanks to an amendment by a local priest.[15] Other dioceses going down this road include Lincoln, Sheffield, Liverpool and Truro. They use different models. Truro envisages clusters of churches as one megaparish, with a single Joint Church Council. Sometimes a Minster model centres worship on a town-centre church, with villages united, who get infrequent services.

The Church Commissioners have a special fund, the Strategic Transformation Fund (which should not be confused with their mission fund, the Strategic *Development* Fund, now renamed the SMMI), to award money for these schemes, most of which goes into the heavy amount of administration such amalgamations cause. So, in Sheffield they were given 'six associate archdeacons, three dedicated building officers, a digital mission adviser, two generous-giving officers, and a programme-support officer to "provide the National Church with evidence of progress"'.[16] £4.92 million was given overall to Sheffield, which now also includes 'Lights for Christ Mission Enablers' and a team to work on 'focal ministry'. A further £1.7 million was awarded to help the transition. The Church Commissioners are spending £45 million overall in the dioceses *to fund amalgamations which will cause further decline*, according to any metric and all available precedents. Yet every nationally promoted scheme still follows a belief in teams as the way forward: 'We need to *stop* working on our own and start working in teams covering bigger areas and focussing on mission and growth' states the new Mission directive from Liverpool, despite all the evidence that this will not lead to increase but decline.[17]

The Church Commissioners gave just under £1 million to transform the 29 parishes in Wigan into seven mission hubs. This was carried out with little consultation, laity being informed that the Church of England is not democratic, and with an immediate loss of several clergy, who resigned rather than implement the changes.[18] The hubs were oddly chosen, with one geographically dispersed unit being decided on the criterion of clergy friendship, and with immense opposition, so that the Church

Commissioners were called in to arbitrate, coming down on the side of the diocese. Reading the many objection letters, which were formerly publicly available, often hand-written by people not used to such procedures, was humbling, as one learnt of lives lived in faithful service to the Church, by ordinary parishioners who felt that their traditions and practices were being destroyed.

Opponents were particularly incensed by the need for paid staff for work formerly done by volunteers, believing such money would be better spent on more priests. Amalgamations make it harder to recruit volunteers: first, because the new roles extend too much beyond their community and secondly because the administration is now an awful lot of work. Needing paid people to do work once performed by volunteers adds a significant cost. In vast amalgamations there is also an added layer of bureaucracy in that parishes now need to work with several levels at once. Where once there was just a Parochial Church Council, now there is a 'Church Council' in the original parish as well as the 'new united PCC' to work with.

In the new Wigan arrangements, the control centre included, besides a team rector, a Core Services Manager, Financial Officer, Funeral co-ordinator, part-time funeral co-ordinator, Grants co-ordinator (fund-raising) and seven part-time co-ordinators for the various mission hubs. Lay people had valued their funeral work as important pastorally and one person with a funeral-direction background reported how distressing it now was for families not to know who would be taking their loved one's service until the last minute, with fewer clergy willing (or with the time) to actually take them.[19] Anecdotal evidence is that the end result of all this has been woeful.

If one needs further proof of the failure of pastoral organization, the Church in Wales is the place to look. Following Lord Harries' Church in Wales Revision Report of 2011, in 2020 the whole province was divided into amalgamations of parishes underwhelmingly entitled, 'Ministry Areas', which could be as large as twenty or so parishes. They were to be served by teams of specialists. The Diocese of Llandaff has the gall to suggest that this is biblical: 'Jesus worked in a team; Ministry

Areas are a return to a more collaborative way of working'.[20] As mentioned earlier, even the Church of England's own document about church closure simplification states that 'anecdotal evidence from Wales suggests a super-parish model has not worked well'.[21] A joint letter from Welsh lay people in the *Church Times* showed that in the Diocese of St Asaph, worshippers were down in just one year from 358 to 245 in Denbigh MA and from 186 to 143 in Maelor MA.[22]

Church Closures

In 2021 there was a proposal to make it easier to close churches, GS2222 or, as it quickly became nicknamed, 'The Church Closers' Charter'. More people wrote in to comment on it than any other piece of legislation about to come to the General Synod and reaction was overwhelmingly negative. For church closures are the other side of pastoral reorganization and they partly fund it. Buildings donated and built by our ancestors, which are ours to steward, are to be denied to later generations for short-term gain. The report revealed plans by dioceses for 368 closures in the next five years, and this was before any revision to the current procedures for enacting closure, which would make such a process easier.[23]

This is one of the most serious ways in which the current leadership betrays the mission of the Church and the heroic attempts by local congregations to keep their (often historic) building in good repair. Parish churches account for 45% of all Grade 1 listed buildings. Once gone, they are gone for ever. An example of the pain this causes can be seen in the working-class former parish of Holy Trinity Millbrook. Not only was this church closed but the offer of the Orthodox parish of St Silouan, who had been using it for some years, to buy it was rejected in favour of a commercial buyer.

Dioceses also fund their shortfall and their reorganization plans by leasing or even selling parsonage houses. Thanks to the impressive work by the Save Our Parsonages organization, they were prevented from selling them off while an incumbent was living there, but in an interregnum and when parishes are merged, they are ripe for the picking. The former director of Save Our Parsonages, Anthony Jennings, writes:

> In the dioceses, buildings are generally seen as a problem rather than an asset, and parsonages are not seen as 'Church buildings' anyway. They are there to be sold off as 'old' and 'outdated'. Indeed, the whole approach of the Church to its heritage seems curiously out of date. Environmentalism and energy saving, too, are interpreted as 'old is bad, new is good', even though the dioceses have had more trouble and expense with badly built 1960s and 1970s houses. This all means no value is placed on the symbolic and practical power of the parsonage in the community, and policy instead favours moving vicars away from the centre of the community and discouraging the social use of the parsonage.[24]

The missional nature of such buildings is ignored. I know two clerics who made full use of their sizeable Lincolnshire rectory for hospitality and events, so that people who might never have come inside the church next door were encouraged by the friendliness of their welcome to lose their fear. They had a toddler group meet there and even in lockdown used the house and garden to film their online dramatic school assemblies, which went viral.

Parish churches themselves are places that speak to people about God even when they are empty. In 2018 the National Churches Trust commissioned a survey, which found that 49% of all adults in Britain visited a church the previous year, which is 25 million people. 24% attended a life event service, 11% were there for religious activity or prayer and 8% to light a candle or be quiet.[25]

Ballooning Diocesan Structures and Loss of Parochial Agency

The pastoral reorganizations and sellings-off described above completely undermine the relation between priest and people and do nothing to render the ministry and mission of the Church more sustainable. It is galling that they are carried out at the same time that diocesan administration grows ever larger. In my own diocese of Southwell 22% of stipendiary posts are diocesan, which is a typical figure, while the Diocese of Winchester has 78 people working in its headquarters, not counting archdeacons and bishops. Oxford diocese boasts four communication officers alone. If one looks at the national figures for 2020, it appears that money for stipends is £363m, with diocesan costs £126m, bishops £38m, Archbishops' Council £32m, cathedrals £20m, Church Commissioners £76m, Pensions £84m, National Costs £15m and a further £49 million on other categories.[26] Front-line ministry accounts for only 45% of the total central spend, which is a wholly bizarre use of money and not one that suggests that the parish (or even the human person) is front and centre of Anglican strategy. Parishes themselves raised £924m in 2020, of which £319 million was donated in parish share and the rest spent on running costs, giving, building works and so on.

Adding bishops and diocesan costs together accounts for just under half of the amount spent on parochial clergy and quite a number of those in stipendiary ministry will be in diocesan posts. It is important to remember that a diocese does not generate money but absorbs it, unlike the parishes that it comprises. When the quota, as it was then called, was instituted in 1915, it was intended to finance the new diocesan offices then beginning to be staffed from the parishes.[27] The first suffragan bishop of Sherwood within the Southwell diocese wrote a poem that recalls his earlier years in the diocese 'when the staff was mostly Margaret Parkes' and 'no-one paid their quota, for / There wasn't one to pay'.[28] It is significant that the diocese of Winchester eschews the word 'parish share' for 'common mission fund', thereby indicating their spending priorities.

Formerly, as already mentioned, many parishes possessed their own resources in the form of glebe land and other endowments. To make more parity between benefices, some of which were richly endowed while others paid poorly, all glebe was taken into diocesan control on the understanding that it would be returned to parishes in the form of stipend. In the Parliamentary debate, even the Second Estates Commissioner who introduced the bill foresaw trouble ahead: 'many people fear – and this matter is especially important in the more rural areas – that if the endowment is taken away, the parish will be more exposed to the risk of pastoral reorganization'.[29] These fears were all too well founded. In 1976, when this measure was passed, about half of all parishes had glebe, including a number in urban areas. Cathedral glebes had been transferred to the Ecclesiastical Commissioners in the nineteenth century and the now Church Commissioners have faithfully funded them, including new sees, ever since. This has, however, not been the case with parishes, whose glebe in diocesan hands is often not well managed.

Stephen Billyeald from the Save the Parish financial scrutiny group has made a special study of the use of glebe by individual dioceses, which they hold in Diocesan Stipendiary Funds. He found that 60% of dioceses are failing to generate a reasonable income from the DSF and 30% of dioceses are failing to make reasonable investment gains on DSF, thus neglecting a very important endowment fund that was put into their care fifty years ago. The seven dioceses using Total Return Accounting (TRA) generate more money for clergy stipends but have made no commensurate reduction in parish share. Oxford diocese has even tried to use DSF money for other purposes, until told that it was illegal. The result of the removal of glebe means that parishes are now expected to pay for their ministry even though their assets have been handed over to the diocese, while cathedrals in the same position were not expected to pay anything.

Strategic Development Funding

Until recently, something called the Darlow formula ensured that poor parishes were supported, but in 2015 a report chaired by John Spence, Finance Chair of the Archbishops' Council, *Resourcing the Future*, claimed that this was a mode of resourcing failure and decline. Instead, money was to be divided between a Strategic Development Fund for missional growth projects, to be competitively organized, and a Lowest Income Communities Funding, which would be organized at diocesan level. A portion of money does go to fund stipendiary clergy in deprived areas from the LICF, but it depends upon the diocese, some of which put the LICF money in a general fund for multiple purposes or use it to pay quota shortfalls.

Ever more money is being required of parishes, even while the Church Commissioners have recently done well financially, with a £500 million extra in 2020 and a similar figure predicted for the next couple of years. We have already seen where this money is going. In particular, £45m is going into hostile pastoral reorganization through the Strategic Transformation Fund. Much more is going into Strategic Development Funding. In 2014–21 £176.7 million was allocated, which went into projects that, as I pointed out in the Introduction, have only 'witnessed' under 13,000 'new disciples' when the target set was 89,000.[30] Even this 13,000 may be over-optimistic, since projects could decide for themselves what constituted a 'new disciple' and the report questioned such vagueness, also stating that figures 'do not always reflect the reality on the ground'.[31]

Very little research has been published about the make-up of the many resource churches created by this fund, but the Church Army is reported as suggesting that 59% of Fresh Expressions are composed of already established Christians from other churches, while a London survey came out with 70% in church plants.[32] When St Matthias Church was taken over by an HTB (Holy Trinity Brompton) plant, one local and growing evangelical church, St Jude's, lost 90% of its teenagers and 30% of its congregation overall, while two thirds of the existing congregation of St Matthias itself decamped, as the style of worship changed out of all recognition.[33]

At the same time as a resource church is typically given half a dozen paid positions, plus administrators, assigned ordinands and curates, parishes around are amalgamated. The resource church usually has no relation whatsoever with the surrounding parishes, but 'resources' them by sending people to start other new congregations. In my own diocese, at least one of Trinity Church in Nottingham's curates aims to plant a new church in a village that already has a church.[34] As the Chote report points out, 'SDF projects are of their nature disruptive to the existing church ecology' and have become lightning rods for feelings of 'lack of trust and the unity of purpose'.[35] A typical resource church is supported by several millions, while parishes are shorn of clergy and put into unwieldy groups set up to fail.

Moreover, until pressure by Save the Parish forced some change, small and rural churches were forbidden from even applying to the SDF. And lest one become too excited by the announcement in 2022 of £1.2 billion in grants over the next three years, only £49 million is for more clergy and 'young leaders', so it is unclear how much of it goes into stipendiary clerical positions, while of the £240 million for 'frontline work' this is still the competitive system of funding growth projects, only with smaller churches now able to bid.

Again, all this comes through dioceses, who must put forward the projects, not directly to parishes. The modest suggestion by Sir James Burnell-Nugent that a tiny portion of the £550 million growth in assets in 2020 by the Church Commissioners – £12 million – be spent to cancel the shortfall in parish finance caused by Covid has fallen on deaf ears.[36] Dioceses are instead lured into making inflated claims for growth in projects that are only funded for five years, thereby aiming for quick and unsustainable increase with a scale of support that makes it almost impossible to appear to fail. The money then stops, which is itself a problematic cut-off point for what is intended to be a long-term project, often with new buildings to sustain.

There are honourable exceptions here, such as the work Exeter Diocese funded through SDF to support pilgrimage and hospitality projects in its mainly rural churches. The excellent practical guide, *How Village Churches Thrive*, is one result of this work. Similarly collaborative and supportive of churches around the whole diocese was Worcester's project with young people. In both cases the amount was relatively small – £1 million for Exeter and less for Worcester – far less than for a single resource church.

But it is also worth realizing that SDF funding comes with a compulsory contribution from the diocese, which can be quite substantial. Leicester's resource churches in 2018 gained £16,176,000, but the diocese had to pay out £5,344,000. This money will normally come from parish share unless the diocese has reserves to draw on – such as glebe land, which was originally parochial! The way some dioceses fund their contribution is through attaching curacies to the resource church, thus giving even more to these favoured places.

While it is quite proper that the Church Commissioners fund mission projects, and the Estates work is particularly important, the evidence so far suggests, first, that SDF projects are not having any appreciable impact in terms of growth, for which they are aimed, and secondly that they are expensive. Thirdly, the whole way in which they are financed and chosen does damage to local churches, who are paying for them out of their parish share and sometimes by the diocese selling off parsonages, which are parish assets, of which the incumbent is the corporation sole. A common trick is for the diocese to keep a benefice in interregnum for a substantial period, thus running it down and making it ever harder for it to sustain its mission. This allows the diocese to save money on the stipend and rent out the parsonage, with the money going into central coffers, but quite frequently this gives them an opportunity to sell off the parsonage altogether, thus ensuring there can never be another resident priest in the parish. Meanwhile parish share often remains the same, or rises.

Another device is to sell the valuable rectory close to the church and community only to buy a cheaper property much further away, with one cleric in Winchester diocese marooned on the wrong side of the M3 from his parish. Some dioceses sell rectory stock while buying a new property for each incoming archdeacon, so he or she may decide where to live. Naturally, such archdeacons are now full-time, without the parochial responsibilities they would once have had.

Yes, we are talking about systematized corruption so endemic that it is barely named and recognized. Christian pastoral care is being plundered for monetary accumulation by a clerical elite bureaucracy whose purposes are either unclear or illusory.

In all this decision-making, by the dioceses or by the centre, there is no evidence that the health and sustainability of the parish system is front and centre of financial allocation or ministerial planning. The very idea that there will be a parallel system of Fresh Expressions/worshipping communities of comparable size to the number of parishes makes no sense unless the parishes are being set up to wither, and the Church of England wishes to change character completely. The unfairness of expecting ever more money from parishes while giving them ever less in terms of clergy and services is egregious, and is bound to cause anger and unhappiness. Cuts fall particularly harshly in the countryside, where two fifths of Anglicans live, compared to one fifth of the population. They have lost their glebe and endowments, are endlessly reorganized into ever less relational units and pay evermore money for less pastoral care. They do not even get to keep all the fees for funerals or weddings, about half of which go to the diocese.

When the entrepreneurial Six Pilgrims parishes in Somerset languished in vacancy with no sight of a new priest, they took matters into their own hands by raising money to get their ancient churches in really good condition, working out how they could support a new priest by relieving him or her of most administration and even raising enough money to buy a new parsonage, lest the diocese try to sell theirs. They then advertised for a house-for-duty priest. You would imagine that Bath and Wells diocese would be delighted at such co-operation between six parishes, but this is not the case. Not only were they not allowed their priest, but they are unilaterally to be joined to an even larger benefice.

Exploiting the Laity

Central to every reorganization proposal from Paul through Tiller to the recent diocesan horrors has been the involvement of lay people. While the Church has long relied on its worshippers for choirs, churchwardens and mutual pastoral care, the laity are now to be regarded as lay ministers, central to the entire working of the new strategy.

The theology for this is laid out in yet another Anglican report, *Setting God's People Free*, which seems to assume that the laity are currently chained up by clergy who wish to keep all authority to themselves and are only waiting for the opportunity to become active ministers and leaders. It claims: 'we are not trying to train up new volunteers to fill the gaps left by declining clergy numbers or make people work even harder to rescue the institutional Church', but the whole force of its programme is to do just that. It claims there is a theological deficit – not, as might fairly be claimed, in resourcing lay people in the biblical and theological riches of our tradition, but in the theology of leadership, so that they might see themselves as directors.[37] There is no mention of the practical burdens that leadership in a church community brings. Yet these arise not just for those on PCCs but impact equally on pioneering missional activities.

Thus, a critique of this approach has to balance recognition of the existing strength of lay contribution with a realism about what strains it can plausibly bear.

A local sports enthusiast told my husband the other day that nearly all our local football and cricket teams are being led and sustained by quite elderly people, aged 50 upwards, not by younger ones. The same is true of any organization you care to name, from ecology groups to politics. People seem to have ever less time to spend in voluntary activities and we more and more depend on the retired to run civil society.

Nonetheless, parishioners already contribute enormously to their wider communities. A report commissioned by the Church of England on social action noted this involvement and questioned too easy a decision that the parish is in decline:

The Church's reach extends well beyond itself by several orders of magnitude with those it directly helps, those it works with and those it simply lets use its buildings. Many in the Church will be surprised by the range of things that the Church itself does, even more outside the Church will be a little astonished at its reach, range and depth.[38]

This community involvement and web of relations is typical of 90% of parishes. It represents not just useful service but the discipleship that *Setting God's People Free* lauds so highly. The Theos report, *Growing Good: Growth, Social Action and Discipleship in the Church of England*, demonstrated the synergy between these elements in Christian practice in urban priority parishes. They enumerated the following as engendering the kind of relationships that might lead to growth: presence, perseverance, hospitality and generosity and participation.[39]

Yet while an increasingly ageing Christian laity are happy to serve their communities and outreach projects, with a remarkable degree of success, the draining of resources through parish share, keeping up buildings and the often-bewildering amount of material and surveys demanded by the diocese puts volunteering at risk. A churchwarden, one rural dean told me, now has to be expert clerk of works and IT manager, which is a challenging combination of roles.

Moreover, volunteers need to be managed and affirmed, which is where the importance of the relation with the parish priest is crucial. *Setting God's People Free* has much to say about empowering lay leadership, but rather less about *supporting* it. It sometimes seems as if it is a fig-leaf for the dearth of clergy and a source of free labour. The language of 'disciples', that has become the norm in Anglican documents, is less the result of a worked-out theology of a lay apostolate and much more a panicked reaction that resents people who are worshippers unless they are focused on mission. 'In church planting there are no passengers', as John McGinley also said in his Myriad Conference seminar, and it sounds quite threatening.[40] Apparently, they no longer also serve who only stand and wait.

We will not bully people into being lights of the world. There

are very many people faithfully serving their church and looking after their neighbours, but who feel completely unloved and
undervalued by this kind of language being used so freely and
thoughtlessly.

Along with the constant calls for money comes this sense that
the congregation are a drain, not a resource, and that there is
something wrong in caring for them. It fits a model of church
delivered via mission area, where laity will be very distant from
their clergy and left on their own pretty much to find a local
lay 'focal minister'. Where such people are to come from, if the
well-being and formation of the parish is not a direct responsibility of anyone, I do not know.

People will make sacrifices and accept scarcity of resources
if they believe we are united by a common purpose and shared
goods. But the present spending priorities of the Church of
England are not fair and equitable. The people in our congregations are our treasure, gifts from God to us, whether they
are wheelchair-bound, infirm or elderly, young and sprightly,
or middle-aged and psychologically burdened. Only when the
Church of England demonstrates with its allocation of resources
that it does value its parishes, and the people who hold them
together, will we flourish.

4

Managerial Mission

Although by its nature the Church is a missionary organization, charged with preaching the good news and baptizing, I had often wondered quite how it was that the noun 'mission' came to dominate the avalanche of Anglican reports and diocesan straplines. It is, as I have already remarked, oddly contentless, unlike the older word, 'evangelism', which suggests we have the good news of the gospel to impart. Historically, its current usage is derived from the world of the nineteenth-century missionary societies and in particular the World Missionary Conference held in Edinburgh in 1910, where missiology is often said to originate.

What I had not realized, until reading Lyndon Shakespeare's brilliant analysis of managerialism, was the importance of the word 'mission' in management theory. Successful managers are 'makers of worlds by the use of words', and those words must have particular qualities: 'low in definition and direct reference, vague and mysterious in terms of precise content, easy to say, vivid and radical sounding in metaphorical and imagistic terms'.[1]

Two key terms theorists employ for such world-making are 'mission' and 'vision', and I need hardly remind my readers of the recent use of these words in the 'Vision and Strategy' documents, as well as the ubiquity of the first term from *Mission-Shaped Church* onwards.

The distinction between the two in management theory is that the vision is what gives the organization direction and meaning, while the mission points to how the organization will realize its purpose, so defined. The ubiquitous mission statement that so oppresses every level of the Church – with the diocese of Winchester under Tim Dakin demanding yearly statements from parishes – is an exercise in vision strategy, but the Church, while embracing managerialism with an unholy hospitality, has confused mission and vision so that mission has displaced the vision to become an end in itself. Every single facet of our lives as Christians is held to be for the sake of mission and is subsumed in utilitarian fashion to this end. We are thus managerial in our evangelistic thought and practice but still worse in a distorted fashion, in that we have put the strategic delivery word, 'mission' in the place of our vision.

Examples of this confusion can be seen in the Mission Action Plans, which are now the norm in all dioceses, which are examples of a central facet of managerialism in practice. In Southwark Diocese, for example, where every parish is obliged to formulate one, they must set themselves targets:

> Action is enabled through SMART goals: we set ourselves goals that are specific, measurable, achievable, resourced and timed. We have a clear plan so we know where we are in relation to the goals we have set ourselves. People have owned our goals and are leading on specific actions: our lay leaders are encouraged and well supported in this.[2]

What renders this managerialism in action is such built-in calculability, with the onus on the 'employee' – here, an emphasis on the laity – to carry out the strategy and be accountable.

Now there is real value in a church community sitting down to audit its strengths and weaknesses and having a close look at the area it serves, as well as planning ahead. The Diocese of Chichester has a less functional version of the Southwark document, with useful advice. The problem lies in the functionalism of the SMART managerial goals, which belong to a profit-making business seeking a growth of market share rather than a church.

And yet, as Justin Lewis-Anthony points out in his critique of ecclesiastical managerialism, as long ago as 1984 management theorists were pointing out the fallacies implicit in such action planning *even* in the case of secular businesses: the fallacy of predetermination, which ignores discontinuities and the unexpected; the fallacy of detachment, in which hard data is abstracted from 'soft' experience; and the fallacy of formalization, which assumes that the reality of an organization can be fully captured by breaking it down into components.[3] SMART criteria were evolved to encourage growth in the business sector, not the aims of the Church of England, but it seems that the latter has not only confused spiritual with monetary growth (innocently or not so innocently?) but has adopted a flawed and perhaps outdated theory of even pecuniary expansion.

One key reason for the downgrading of parochial life is precisely the embrace of managerialism and SMART criteria for success. By this, I do not mean that the Church should not be well managed, but that we have embraced the goals and techniques of managerial*ism* (and technically questionable techniques at that) as an unquestioned ideology. The key aims of management as a secular science are efficiency, predictability, control and accountability. They become managerialism when they act as a form of social control that shapes a social body.[4]

Stephen Pattison dates managerialism's advent in Church circles to George Carey's pre-enthronement interview in 1991, where he said he wanted the Church to be run more like a business, arguing that Jesus was a management expert.[5] The kind of managerialism that now obtains is more 'new wave', privileging the consumer, and the manager as an inspirer, who provides the vision, which his or her employees will then instantiate through producing new efficiencies. The analogies with the model of megaparishes under a team leader and the lay volunteers to carry out the work are strong and not accidental.

Along with an optimism about the employee's ability to carry out the vision and strategy through SMART criteria comes a trust in measurable outcomes, which supposedly show the true worth of an activity. The targets set of 'witnessing disciples' in SDF funding awards are a clear example of such calculability and the stress of meeting them means that what constitutes a disciple can mean merely someone who turns up to a café with a final prayer or at a youth gaming session. Pattison notes how attractive such a strategy is in organizations with limited resources and is clear that care is needed if the Church is not to substitute sub-goals such as control and calculability for its ultimate aims, which are eschatological. Our purpose as the body of Christ is to worship God and bring the whole world to union with him, but these goals can be easily lost once measurable targets take centre stage.

The parish, in particular, is a form of organic life with its own local specificities that are like no other, and a porosity that is resistant to targets. Its laity are primarily parishioners, not disciples, the term now preferred by the hierarchy, not because of the Bible, but because this is to involve the 'employees' in the success of the business operation: 'human subjects are exhorted to expand and intensify their contribution as "human resources" in order to enhance production, maximize value, thus leading the organization to success'.[6] While these are instrumental values for competitive triumph, they are couched even in the secular world in the quasi-religious language of mission and vision and so prove all too seductive for the Church, where they serve to conveniently mask a secular-derived instrumentality allowing an apparently convenient marriage of pietism with the latest slick techniques

This functionalism is, however, all too clear in some diocesan straplines, for example: 'Called Together: grow, enrich, resource'; 'Discovering God's Kingdom, Growing the Church'; 'Bigger Church to Make a Bigger Difference'; 'Growing in God'.[7] The last has implicit within it some theology of participation and formation, but the others seem primarily focused on purely numerical growth, especially when one burrows down to their sub-clauses. While it would be good to see a reversal of the declining numbers of worshipping Christians, these visions have succumbed to growth rather than faithfulness as the primary aim.

It is significant, to say the least, that, despite the relentless emphasis on expansion, the employment of managerial techniques, and their universal roll-out with generous financial resources behind them, the expected growth has not occurred. Indeed, the resource churches with their lavish provision of personnel have not met their expected targets at all and have to the contrary fallen far short.

One key reason is that the decline in churchgoing is the fruit of much larger changes in society, to do with demographic shifts, cultural degradation, changes in lifestyle and the decline of all communal activities and institutions, including pubs. Although, at the profoundest level, this weakening of the bonds of love may indeed be to do with secularization, it is also the case that secularization, in the narrower sense of a decline in religious participation, is but one example of this broader collapse of community belonging: the 'bowling alone' phenomenon first identified in the United States by Robert Putnam.[8]

So, although the Archbishop of York told the Save the Parish conference in July 2022 that 'if we led more Christ-like lives, then we would see our churches flourish', it is just not that simple. All businesses that need actual people to come through the door are struggling and the Church is no exception. The new resource churches tend just to redistribute Christians and attract only modest numbers of wholly new converts.

Why Ecclesiastical Managerialism Will Fail

Apart from wider social forces, there is another reason why the SMART goals and growth approaches fail, which is that they misunderstand the very nature of the Church. For managerialism does not distinguish between different sorts of bodies:

> The central doctrine of managerialism is that the differences between such organizations as, for example, a university and a motor vehicle company, are less important than the similarities, and that the performance of all organizations can be optimized by the application of generic management skills and theory. It follows that the crucial element of institutional reform is the removal of obstacles to 'the right to manage'.[9]

We are seeing the dangers of this sort of approach in the National Health Service, which is more ruled by managers than doctors, and in the university sector, where SMART criteria are destroying liberal education and turning it increasingly into a consumer product, or in the police force where it is resulting in mostly unsolved or even uninvestigated crimes. What the NHS, universities and the police have in common with the Church of England is that they are all teleologically purposive institutions, with their own internal traditions of practice, expertise and values developed over time. Martyn Percy wrote that 'the church is not a body that is supposed to be ever more productive, like a factory or industry that simply improves its output from year to year. It is an organic body of wisdom, in which pruning, seasons, life and death, course through its very veins.'[10]

One helpful way of considering how different a body the Church is from a business is to think of it in terms of Alasdair MacIntyre's idea of a practice, or as a series of such practices. In *After Virtue,* he describes a practice as an activity that has goods intrinsic to it:

> Any coherent and complex human activity through which goods internal to that form of activity are realized in the course of trying to achieve those standards of excellence which are appropriate to and partially definitive of, that form of activity, with the result that human powers to achieve excellence and human conceptions of the ends and goods involved, are systematically extended.[11]

His first example is playing chess. A child may play to win or even cheat but only if he or she decides to submit to the game and learn its techniques and strategies will the child become a good player and even extend the possibilities of the game. MacIntyre's second example is portrait-painting, where he develops further the way that a practice has within it the possibility of a mode of life, which develops historically, as new painters come along who see creative extensions of the practice, but only by first learning its rules and goods.

He distinguishes the practice from the institution that might be related to it: the chess club or the Royal Academy in his two examples. The institution may nurture and promote the practice but might offer extrinsic goods, such as prizes, and can even corrupt the practice, as when all that matters to the chess-players is competition, rather than the worth of their play. Managerialism infecting and corrupting Church policy is one example of an institution losing touch with its practices. But practices are conversely sustained by institutions and MacIntyre believes it was the practice of moral enquiry and debate within universities that nurtured a wider sense of the public realm. He also believes that by virtuous practices within institutions the ravages of consumer capitalism may be resisted, since they are always open to the common good and improving human excellence as such. It is a virtuous circle of virtue: genuine institutions are constituted by practices, but institutional structures are required to nurture and protect them.

The Church then is both a series of practices and an institution. The practices are the sacraments: the life of prayer, reconciliation, service and so on. MacIntyre's terminology reveals that, in one sense, the practices *are* the Church, as she operates as the body of Christ, so that the Church is an active body. That is one reason why the managerial model fails so utterly to capture her life. (I deliberately employ the feminine pronoun for the Church to avoid this functionality.)

In this respect, we can contrast a genuine institution with a mere *organization*. As Lyndon Shakespeare demonstrates, the managed organization body has no intrinsic life because it ignores the embodied nature of human persons, whom it reduces to 'rational agents who make choices through means/ ends formulae, based on "utility" criteria or "general value" orientation'.[12] This is the anthropology that undergirds the privileging of Fresh Expressions in *Mission-Shaped Church*, as we analysed it in *For the Parish*.[13] A managed organization is a machine in the Cartesian sense of an automaton in which the actual agent is overlooked or viewed as a mere functional item.[14]

In the same way, an organization is extrinsically focused on its goals rather than the manner of their achieving as being integral to their genuine achievement. As Remi Jardat puts it:

An organization has to do with 'coordination of persons and things in order to exert determined functions', whereas an institution consists in a 'normative complex', whose principal elements. are 'aims of a higher order', 'foundation by rules which have force of law (are valid for everyone)' and are characterized by a high stability.[15]

An institution like the Church has a higher aim or *telos* than an organization, and the ways in which it goes about achieving those aims have value in themselves and persist over time. Custom and ethos are normative modes of action and determine behaviour in ways that are not purely functional but have an entelechy, focused on the good, on our calling to life in God. The current mission strategy, with its commitment to 'a diverse *smorgasbord*' of culture and church embodiment, and its mixed ecology, is trying to do mission in a functional way which denies the specificity of these practices and believes it can put any old cultural content in their place.[16]

Parochial Life as a Practice

Parochial life is already a practice in MacIntyre's use of the word. It is a mode of life with its own internal goods and excellencies, such as a common liturgical life, exercises of reconciliation, and service to the community. It exists within a tradition of such work. As MacIntyre writes, 'to enter into a practice is to enter into a relationship not only with its contemporary practitioners but also with those who have preceded us in the practice'.[17] To worship at a local church is to be part of a long sequence of faithful people and to be aware also of those coming after us. The care of the building itself fosters such an understanding. It helps to render intelligible the life that goes on there in the present. Thus, the various activities of parish life and worship above all nourish and develop the virtues and excellencies of their participants. This is not to idealize the parish – though it is noticeable how saying anything positive about parish life is likely to be so viewed in ways that are not the case with any other activity or group. It is merely to indicate what sort of practice it is: a quest for the good life, for holiness. Whether the parishioners are cooperative and helpful or sticky and negative that quest remains and is articulated by what happens week by week.

To make such a mode of life flourish will not happen through treating it functionally and by organizational centralization. The dioceses who try this will fail. Indeed, the Episcopal Church in the United States has been employing managerial mission now for fifty years and there has been steady numerical decline. For once one turns an institution and series of practices into a purely functional organization, one loses the teleological and so the institutional *raison d'être*. Of course, this must be *a fortiori* true of the Church. And a genuine *telos* is not just a future goal, but one that already shapes the whole life of the one pursuing it. The means – the practices – are not separate from the end vision but are already intrinsic to it, already the goal in miniature like a plant within the seed.

Centralization and Functionalism

We see the loss of teleology in the Church of England in the cult of mission for mission's sake and in the incoherence of projects like 'Vision and Strategy'. It is indicative of the functionalism that the archbishops employ that the managerial 'world-building' concepts form the very title for the project where there should be content supplied to the vision and strategy. In view of this inversion, one has to conclude that the ecclesial substitution of means for ends is even more complete than in the secular versions. Perhaps that is unsurprising: the Church as a sacred body has more fully sacralized the very purposelessness of our secular society. In this way it acts as a legitimating civil religion. But that is no longer Christianity.

When vision *is* spoken of in 'Vision and Strategy', instead of making conversion and union with Christ the aim of evangelism, the vision is for Church people to be 'Jesus-shaped' and 'Christ-centred' so that the vision is ironically internal to the Church rather than focused on outreach. The message here is also somewhat confused, in that one is to be shaped by 'Jesus' and also by 'the five marks of mission'. This shaping, which could have constituted a genuine *telos*, is in reality purely instrumental, because it exists to prepare the disciples to carry out the aims, which are not eschatological but SMART: doubling the numbers of children and young people by 2030, ten thousand new churches/worshipping congregations.

Taglines such as 'simpler, humbler, bolder' conflict with the complexity of adding a whole new parallel system of ten thousand new communities to the parish church system, almost rivalling its 12,500 parishes in size. Protestations that this will make no difference to the parish system are nonsensical, since such a parallel separate network of communities is necessarily in competition with the parishes, and its worshipping communities are openly presented as alternatives.

You could, of course, start a new congregation in an existing parish, where its reach has hitherto not been effective and that community might be strong enough to achieve the status of a parish church and pay its share, but generally such communities are quite small and fragile, highly dependent on the current leadership, and make much more sense as parish mission projects, where the stability of the parish can be a support. It is noticeable that all the examples of good practice in the Estates Task Group podcasts work with a parish church.

These instrumental aims are really the supposed 'vision' element; yet there is precious little about the strategy for achieving such immense goals. So, we have an instrumentalized conception without even a thinking through of the instruments. Much supposedly hangs upon the transformation of all Christians into 'missionary disciples'. From other documents this means that lay people are to lead many of the new worshipping communities, drive evangelism and produce more of these youthful participants. Yet there is a mismatch between wholly centralized decision-making and the fact that it is to a large part reliant on volunteers on the ground who have to carry it out, with little say in the strategy.

The Church has become much more centralized in decision-making since the Turnbull Report of 1995, *Working as One Body*, created the Archbishops' Council. This body replaced the Standing Committee of the General Synod, which contained eighteen elected lay and clerical members. Instead, the Council became more like a cabinet, with many people appointed by the archbishops; out of seventeen members, only eight to represent the clergy and laity, with the rest either bishops or the archbishops' nominees. The funding streams from the Church Commissioners are decided, and their direction given by the Council, so that although they may often say that power is devolved to the dioceses, this is in considerable measure a disguise for the centralizing transfer of power from parish to diocese and then from diocese to the centre.

In this respect, Strategic Transformation Funding seems to follow a similar pattern everywhere, as we have already seen with the ubiquity of Mission Action Plans. The same documents laying out principles of pastoral organization are circulated in the various dioceses. And while such documents tend routinely to claim that subsidiarity rules, and it is individual parishes who must decide the nature of their future, the centre trumps the role of both parish and diocese. Thus the Diocese of Liverpool claims to believe 'that those who live in the community are usually in the best position to identify what may work best for that community. Therefore, the Diocese prefers to take a bottom-up process with recommendations emerging from the deanery in consultation with the parishes and interested parties.'[18] But this is swiftly followed by the intervention of the Mission and Pastoral Committee who will 'ensure that any deanery proposals are in harmony with Diocesan policy'. [19] And we all know where 'diocesan policy' derives from.

An even more egregious example can be found in the Diocese of Truro's plans to close churches and amalgamate parishes in East Wivelshire. The document blandly states 'we are to grasp this God inspired vision with enthusiasm. The Steering Group has adopted this vision believing it to be the way God is asking us to grow, therefore it is important to note we are not seeking opinions on God's given Vision'.[20] The authoritarian confidence in the infallibility of this group is beyond papal. Perhaps this is to plug a credibility gap, since it suggests that God sends a vision to close churches. The new groupings are, moreover, not named for anything locally meaningful, such as names of the many Cornish saints, but rather coyly and insultingly: 'alpha, bravo and charlie'.

There is now a further Governance Review, which claims to simplify the national administrative structures, and which will, in effect, centralize power even further. It includes some mention of decentralization, but it is hardly encouraging:

> **Focus on the true purpose** – in this case serving the Church. Allocating sufficient attention to the Church's activities (Campbell and Goold's 'Market Advantage test').
> **Appropriate levels of subsidiarity** – adding value to the cure of souls at local level by recognizing and delivering those activities best done nationally to maximize strategic or economic value (the 'Parenting Advantage test').[21]

Instead of looking at theological ideas of subsidiarity, the review relies on management theorists Michael Goold and Andrew Campbell, for whom 'market advantage' – finding where you score over your competitors – and 'parental advantage' – identifying where the central body's strategies and roles should concentrate, are seen in wholly economic terms, as is clear from 'adding value to the cure of souls', which is so inappropriate a use of language that it is hard not to weep. The point is that the notion of subsidiarity as presented discovers curiously little that is best done at local level (in total contrast to the approach of Catholic Social Teaching), while the language of 'parenting' is somewhat patronizing.

The theological opening of the review denies that management criteria are appropriate, but then the main body of the document goes blithely on its managerial way, and no one is deceived. Interestingly, the review makes its own distinction between organization and institution:

> Organizations and Institutions are not the same thing. The former is a structure designed to deliver a known goal; the latter is a complex organism intended to hold together the interplay of different but related interests. The second description fits the Church of England: a complex collection of divergent and overlapping interests and activities.[22]

Yet this is not a teleological view of an institution, which is not a holding together of divergent interest groups, rather like the American constitution, but instead a seeking of the Common Good by embedded practices and traditions. It will include debate within it about how best to recognize and exercise its practices, but as a divine institution *in esse* there is a *common* good for us all. Our shared interests as human creatures are not divergent.

Centralization can also be seen in a confidential briefing paper for the College of Bishops in September 2021, which revealed plans for something oddly akin to the structure of the Roman Curia, proposing bishops without any people to shepherd, but instead national 'portfolios' such as 'Brexit Bishop' or 'Covid Bishop'.[23] There were also proposals passed in the July 2022 General Synod, heavily promoted by the Archbishops' Council, in relation to the election of an Archbishop of Canterbury by more people from the worldwide Anglican community and fewer from the diocese of Canterbury, which encourage the holder of this position to see him or herself as quasi-papal in relation to leadership of the Communion, which is a wholly dispersed and loose grouping, that really does not need such a figure. If such a post were necessary, it could be filled by rotation by Primates from the different continents.

So out of all this centripetal activity, we have mission, vision and strategy emerging directly from the archbishops and presented to the rank and file as a *fait accompli*, which, against a backdrop of clergy cuts and pastoral reorganization, they will be expected somehow to 'deliver'. And although we have quite an undefined sense of what *content* is to be delivered, there is a very clear indication that it is growth itself, which has been turned into the aim of the gospel. The situation is well summarized by Darrell Guder:

> The more the Church is treated as an organization, the more its mission becomes focused on techniques designed to maximize output and productivity. We become obsessed with quantity instead of quality, and where we have a care for quality, it is only to serve the larger goal of increasing quantity.

The Church moves to becoming a managed machine, with its managers judging their performance by growth-related metrics.[24]

These are the words of a theologian at the very heart of missional theology, who has promoted it as a central focus of ecclesiology for many years through the Gospel and our Culture Network.

Exploiting the Laity Again

Everything in this managerial mission depends on the 'employees' and here we have a real problem. For the people who become vital for a church that has (out of no financial necessity) drastically cut its clergy and turned many of the few that it has left into managers rather than ministers, are the laity – who are not employees. You cannot force them or direct them to do anything. Indeed, they pay heavy parish shares and could even be regarded as the employers.

And yet, as I have already indicated in Chapter Two, the influence of 'religionless Christianity' over many years means that these same people are undervalued, even though they keep the ecclesial show on the road to a very great extent. We need to reverse direction here. The Church is not going to gain missionary disciples by treating the current worshippers as irrelevancies and a diversion from time better spent on mission in (now rather imaginary) urban jungle wilds.

Contradictorily, the laity are derided on the one hand as a cultural rump, while on the other hand they are at the heart of the new 'Emerging Church' strategies. The report *Setting God's People Free*, commissioned by the Archbishops' Council, claims that 'the task we face as the Church is not a functional or managerial one. We are not trying to train up new volunteers to fill the gaps left by declining clergy numbers or make people work even harder to rescue the institutional Church.'[25] Yet that is precisely what the strategy seems to be. It is wholly clear from the report that it is far less interested in how one might live out the lay apostolate as, say, a good Christian accountant or care worker, than in how the laity can be harnessed to provide ministry and mission in purely ecclesial terms:

> Until laity and clergy are convinced, based on their baptismal mutuality, that they are equal in worth and status, complementary in gifting and vocation, mutually accountable in discipleship, and equal partners in mission, we will never form Christian communities that can evangelize the nation.[26]

Mission is the aim here and there are a number of references to 'lay leadership' as well as a story that delights in the fact that a diocese has lost twelve stipendiary clergy but gained forty paid lay ministers. Quite why these paid ministers are not to be ordained is not made clear.

This is not to say that lay people do not do pastoral care or share in taking services, especially as Readers, but they are lay, not clergy, called mainly to serve God in the secular world, whereas this report cannot really make up its mind what a lay person actually is. It calls for more theology, but again this seems to consist of more support for the idea of lay leadership. It is, however, quite dismissive of Reader training and has precious little to say about Reader ministry. This is, no doubt, because it is not seen to be missional enough in its focus. Again, the laity are to be released purely for the great idol: mission – a notion that, as we have seen, derives from management manuals rather than from the New Testament.

I am sure the report is correct to point to clergy who do not use lay people effectively. We are also not really served by our Synodical structures, which favour people with time and money. We would do much better to confine Synod to necessary legislation and have supplementary meetings in dioceses on a Sunday to which anyone can turn up: something more like the informal synods arising across the Roman Catholic Church, which are more like people's councils or 'soviets' as those bodies were originally intended. What we do not want are paid lay ministers who lack the training we expect of clergy, which is really a device to gain ministry on the cheap. There will be suitable candidates among parishioners for modes of ordained ministry, again properly trained and equipped.

Yet the problem is that although *Setting God's People Free* endorses sharing training and teaching with lay people, this never seems to be for the sake of the value of what is to be communicated. It always has to be functional: to enable 'mission' that operates in a kind of futile circle: the point of numbers is to generate more numbers, as if the real aim were truly only money and empty power. Again, we come round on the carousel of managerial mission in which the mode of delivery has become the purpose, as if we were really confronted with a sort of collectivized version of the Prosperity Gospel.

The Anglican-derived Methodist movement and the Evangelical Revival, like the Oxford Movement, were, by contrast, all aflame with faith: faith in the power and truth of the gospel. It was their various rediscoveries of gospel truths that drove the leaders of those movements and inspired people. Recalling this, it is not arrogant to suggest that the Christian faith and our Anglican charism has something to offer our fast-disintegrating culture. If we do not think that is true, there is no point to our existence as a Church.

We are, however, saddled, on top of the managerialism I have been describing, with two inadequate and conflicting ecclesiologies, which between them drive these various policy initiatives and endless reports: a marketized evangelicalism on the one hand, and religionless Christianity, which has now become 'contextual theology', on the other. It is to the conflict between these, with the parish church caught in the middle, that I shall now turn.

5

The Parish Between Church Planting and Pioneer Ministry

The ecclesiology that 'Vision and Strategy' and the whole Renewal and Reform agenda promotes is the 'mixed ecology', for which the Church of England is conceived as a rich tapestry of parishes, chaplaincies, Fresh Expressions and plants, all mutually flourishing. The phrase 'mixed ecology' is a rebranding of Rowan Williams' term, 'mixed economy', which Andrew Davison and I critiqued in *For the Parish*.[1] More recently, Anderson Jeremiah attended to its economic and competitive implications:

> Predominantly, it is about utility maximization, and is growth- and success-orientated. The mixed economy combines both a socialist and capitalist approach to the economic market-place, while simultaneously permitting private producers or companies to engage in production and competition in the marketplace.
>
> The mixed economy protects private property over the common good. It allows for supply and demand to determine prices in a neo-liberal, free-market fashion, and privileges economic transactions that are driven by private self-interest and incentives. By allowing competition, a mixed-economic model facilitates innovation and efficiency, where the most efficient succeed. Those who cannot compete will be either bought out or pushed out of the market.[2]

In Bishop Rowan's original usage, he was thinking of the combination of public and private in initiatives such as building hospitals, or even of an economy with public and private money.

Yet he surely did not intend to invoke the neo-liberal competitiveness Jeremiah discerns (it would conflict with his entire social vision). Others did, however, realize those implications, which were manifestly implied in practice, and Angela Tilby therefore came up with a revision – 'mixed ecology' – because a mixed ecology is co-operative and helps every element to thrive. Yet as Jeremiah points out, this unfortunately, like some overly technocratic version of a Green future, just masks the still-continuing economic model, with its emphasis on success, multiplication, and growth and above all, competition.

This chapter will explore two different strains within 'mixed ecology': 'church planting' and 'pioneer ministry' and the ecclesiology that undergirds them. Both, in their different ways, have parochial elements, but as we shall see, what is left out of each works to hollow out the nature of faith and together they do not promote a sustainable ecosystem.

The Church Planting Model

As church planters are quick to point out, new churches have been planted from the New Testament onwards, so that there is no reason why new ones should not be grown today. The problem is that under the present system church planting is, in the main, linked directly to the managerial growth missiology. Like the mixed economy, it also imports competition into what had been a mutually supportive system.

The Centre for Community and Theology published a report concerning five church plants in East London, which on the whole developed good relations with the host congregation, although in the case of two churches the Eucharist now had to be presided over by a priest without vestments at a time when this was illegal, and which would have been a practice quite alien and disturbing to the original congregations.[3] Moreover, between 73% and 80% of those attending these plants were already practising Christians, so some churches somewhere were losing members. This points to the fact that Church planters all too rarely start a church where there was little provision before, and instead 'transplant' or 'infuse'; they take over an existing church with an actual, albeit 'declining' congregation.

The practice is often all-too-imperialist, with the incoming plant choking what life remained, especially when an Anglo-Catholic or middle-of-the-road church is taken over by an evangelical plant. In Portsmouth, for example, the new Harbour Church took over two existing parishes and according to the diocese's own report, lost the congregations that had been worshipping there.[4] Save the Parish was contacted by an Anglo-Catholic church in Winchester diocese, where merging with an evangelical resource church was about to be their fate, even though they had quite a youthful demographic in the small but committed congregation that had managed to survive the deliberate running-down of a lengthy interregnum.

In theory, a transplant into an existing church should attend to and respect the original tradition and its liturgical tradition, but this is rarely the case. At best, a cleric from the new dispensation will half-heartedly preside at a Eucharist they have little understanding of at a very early hour of the day – too early often for the elderly who rely upon it – with the main non-liturgical offering occupying the mid-morning slot. At worst, it just seems to disappear or be corralled into a small room, as in the case of one plant in the West Country where the church has been stripped of holy things, which are now in some kind of indigenous people's reservation, where the original priest carries on trying to celebrate the Eucharist in the tiny space available.

One key element of church planting is that which is funded by the Church Commissioners and the dioceses through Strategic Development Funding (now Strategic Mission and Ministry Investment), in the form of what are called 'resource churches'. These have to be bid for competitively and thus fit the mixed economy model quite precisely. Some take over existing parish churches, while others are bought a former restaurant or auction house; quite often they are situated very close to already existing parish churches and are evidently in competition with them – a one-sided competition insofar as the plant is well-funded and awash with ministers, in contrast to the beleaguered ordinary local clergy. It is hard not to succeed with the size of resources such plants are awarded, which is partly the thinking behind the strategy. They are there to prove that numerical growth is only possible through such novel means. And they are too lavishly resourced to fail. They are intended to 'resource' by getting so large they plant new churches.

Many church plants, whether transplants into another church, or new resource churches, derive from the mission-endeavour of Holy Trinity Brompton. A church plant such as St Augustine Queensgate becomes renamed: 'HTB Queensgate' and although its former choral musical tradition is allowed to continue, its 'indigenous' programme of services, music list or parish life were until recently invisible on the HTB website, although now the service as Communion has been advertised by a link, but there is still no detail. It has been subsumed into their brand identity where all other services are advertised without regard for the diurnal liturgical round just by timings, and where the status of the ministers is unclear. None of this constitutes authentic Anglican practice on any model of churchpersonship. At the former Chinese restaurant, now Nelson Street resource church in Rochdale, you will search in vain for any reference to Holy Communion, baptism or how to arrange a funeral. All that work is presumably left to the vicar in charge of four churches that cover the rest of Rochdale, her ecclesiastical 'Happy Valley'.

Such a marketized method as adopted by HTB instead fits all-too beautifully with the managerial mission outlined in the last chapter. As Martyn Percy notes in a study of the megachurch in the American context:

> A belief in a mechanistic theology in which programme[s] centred on effectiveness and growth are more or less guaranteed, provided principles are discerned and closely applied, will lead to a particular kind of efficient and success-orientated church – and most likely result in some kind of expression of megachurch.[5]

Holy Trinity Brompton is one such, with a huge congregation and scores of ministers serving them. Its success lies in its application of a series of programmes and activities that allow

middle-class professionals to network and make good friendships and in the emotional high that its professional soft rock
music promotes, following the Vineyard style of worship
promulgated by John Wimber, who had a strong influence on
the development of HTB.

Its most successful programme is the Alpha Course, which
has been copied the world over and more recently has been
adapted in an ecumenical direction to embrace use by Roman
Catholics, with the session on the Church even including a sight
of Pope Francis and an interview with a Charismatic Catholic
bishop. Nicky Gumbel has been influenced by Catholic spirituality and makes extensive use of C. S. Lewis in his materials, so
that Alpha is now acceptable to very many sorts of Christian
groups. Its format is also truly inspired in that it involves a meal
and small group discussion, suggesting a sense of openness and
collaboration, while bonding the participants. The weekend
away further deepens the sense of belonging.[6]

The problem with HTB as an ecclesial model is that despite
the orthodox and even Catholic usability of the Alpha Course,
it is not discernibly Anglican. It may inhabit beautiful Anglican
buildings, but it works against their architecture, putting the
worship band and screen in front of the altar, which is just
ignored. Worship accordingly follows the Wimber pattern of a
long series of worship songs, alternating between the affective
and the more stirring 'raising up' God's sovereignty mode, taking
up about half the service, followed by a short prayer time and
a long sermon.

Although the sermon will usually take the form of exegesis
of a verse of Scripture and make much wider biblical reference,
there is often no Bible reading as such: something that would
have astonished earlier generations of evangelicals. There is no
attempt even to hold to the structure of Common Worship and
the service does not usually include a Lord's Prayer or blessing.
There might be some expression of regret, but no formal con-
fession is uttered and no recital of the creed.

Nothing more different from parochial Anglican liturgy can
be imagined because there is no call and response, little congregational involvement in intercession or reading, and precious little

congregational singing, because this is carried by the worship group while the people in the congregation (who are sometimes in the dark as if at the cinema or theatre), move and respond individually to the music, somewhat in the manner of an audience at a pop festival. Those who come seeking ordination from such a liturgical diet will be totally at sea in the parish setting, where worship is more dialogic, more communal, much richer of content and, of course, will follow common Anglican liturgy.

In character HTB worship is also relentlessly upbeat, which is both a strength that can render the Alpha Course a good basic introduction to Christianity, and yet a limitation, in that it does not speak into the difficulties, suffering, tragedies and failures of human life, except in order to recount rescue from them by conversion, with the hint of a more successful life-course to ensue in the future. There is not the drama of the liturgical year with its darker periods of Lenten discipline and lament. Indeed, there is little of the liturgical year at all.

While HTB is careful not to explicitly embrace the prosperity gospel, a major proponent, Joyce Meyer, addressed their leadership conference. HTB comes close to it in some talks, so sure it is that God's blessing will rest on those who follow Christ, in contrast to the many saints who have insisted that God's gifts to us may include an intensified yet redemptive suffering of wrongs. This positivity is one key factor in its success, along with the small groups that engender friendship among like-minded people of one's own age and background, which reinforce the prevailing upbeat tone and ambience. Yet it makes it hard when churches do not succeed, because failure in such a superbly run organization, whose website is dizzyingly fast and well structured, whose every element of presentation is honed and perfectly professional, is really unthinkable. A thoughtful doctoral thesis by an HTB sympathizer (and product), Rich Moy, interviewed church planter leaders and found that those who had experienced loss of numbers after early success really struggled, because in this massively successful enterprise, growth is assumed, and lack of success suggests a lack of faith.[7]

Advised and supported in applications by HTB's own support organization, the Church Revitalization Trust, this model is being rolled out in very large numbers of plants and resource churches. The Church Commissioners' money is thus being spent on a form of church that has no links with Anglican liturgy and practice, or even, arguably, belief. Holy Communion gets a quick aside as something one might do at church in the 'What is Church?' Alpha video, but most HTB churches do not advertise it and neither do many resource churches. It may happen, but how and where remains a mystery from their communications. Furthermore, it is unclear within these churches just who is ordained or not: they frequently do not say.

What is more, the married couple as a ministerial unit sometimes masks an ecclesial practice of male headship, with women confined to teaching children or other women. As Rich Moy writes, 'Although many/most of the larger churches are presented as being co-led by a couple in ministry, it is usually the man who has the theological training, title and ordination.'[8] There is no preservation or use of the charism of ministerial orders and, if ordination of women is formally accepted, it is sometimes because priesthood is seen as not mattering at all. So, whereas many of those who feel unable to accept female ordination on theological grounds fully embrace female equality in general, that is by no means clear in the case of many church plants. In this way, for all the liberal talk of 'inclusivity', an official embrace of gender equality is being covertly undermined, with full official encouragement and ample amounts of financial backing. Such incoherence is what tends to ensue when theology is altogether ignored.

To compound this picture, in many plants and resource churches there appears, anecdotally, at least, to be little or no appetite for missional work through the occasional offices. One senior diocesan cleric suggested to me that in churches in the HTB mould in his own diocese, in defiance of the canons, funerals are only taken for members of the congregation, with baptisms or marriages offered only for committed believers from within the worshipping body. If that were true, it may well be in defiance of Canon Law.[9] Some resource church websites make no mention of the possibility of baptism at all, even though bringing new Christians to the font is surely their *raison d'être.* At HTB central, there is reference to baptism on the website, but you have to sign up to say which service you attend to even start the process, in tacit opposition to the traditional insistence that baptism requires only the minimum of assent (or only the assent of one's parents in the case of babies) since it is the very opening to a new life. A traditional evangelical church like All Souls Langham Place, by contrast, does overtly say on its website that occasional offices are offered to all in the parish, holding to the pastoral tradition that I discerned in the evangelical revival in the nineteenth century.

Generally, in this planting/resource church model, the central parochial work of the cure of souls is just not valued or practised: in complete ignoring of the New Testament, especially the book of Acts. I was told by a priest recently that in most parishes in his predominantly evangelical diocese funeral ministry had more or less dried up, outside the immediate congregation. Funeral Directors knew better than to even ask.

It was noteworthy that in a 2022 round of restructuring in Church House, the Life Events team was closed down, while Vision and Strategy enabling was encouraged happily on its way. Anyone within parish ministry will affirm the enormous missional potential of the occasional offices and yet the centre shows its disdain by not even maintaining the oversight of this work within a district department and by making the Life Events head redundant.

Rich Moy's thesis on HTB history and theology also reveals key facts about its finance. He notes that

> Despite an 'Electoral Roll' [church membership] of over 4000 people, and central church funding for ten 'planting curates', HTB's contribution to central church funds in 2019 through the Parish Share was just £250,000 (although its contributions to the development of Church of England life through its own mechanism 'The Church Revitalization Trust' are much greater).[10]

What is being financed on a massive scale, despite HTB paying, like Amazon in relation to public tax, disproportionately little share to Church finances, is a model of the Church that does not value Anglican teaching, Anglican orders, Anglican liturgy, Anglican sacraments and the occasional offices and cure of souls. It has hollowed out anything recognizably distinctive as Anglican ecclesiology, while operating, in the case of HTB, as a Church within a Church, a posh 'Militant Tendency', with sometimes its own dedicated ordinations.

Rules that obtain for other parishes are ignored in the case of HTB. The resignation of Nicky Gumbel was not followed by the usual interregnum, despite the numbers of experienced clergy who could have carried the church and offered leadership. The new rector was appointed immediately. And it is not unusual for an HTB appointee to a resource church to be directly appointed by the bishop rather than go through an open and competitive application process. In the case of Basingstoke in Winchester Diocese, the new rector was an NSM curate of only one year's experience and again a bishop's appointee.

There is even now a bishop for church planting, Ric Thorpe, who was formerly a lay worship leader at HTB and church planter in London. He is coincidentally head of the Gregory Centre for Church Multiplication or Myriad, where John McGinley announced the 10,000 lay-led worshipping communities. Ric Thorpe led the apologies after that debacle and was presumably behind Myriad's statement soon after: 'We do not think that priests or parishes are limiting factors, and we are not proposing that we divert resources away from them. In fact, the proposal that lay people can be supported in leading new worshipping communities relies on ordained leaders with theological and pastoral understanding.'[11] The nature of this clerical role, however, is described elsewhere in the Myriad literature as one of 'championing'.

This still leaves lay people leading the new worshipping communities, which must necessarily lack sacramental worship. It also fits uncomfortably with statements commended in Myriad's own report, in which lay leaders felt 'unable to fulfil the work that God had called them to', because of a perceived 'lack of authority', and encountered 'structures of oversight and accountability that felt heavy and ill-fitting for the agile and responsive models of mission that their teams wished to express'.[12] This quotation articulates a tension between a personal sense of calling and ecclesial authority. The full report notes that some lay leaders expressed frustration that they could not administer the sacraments themselves.[13] One barely has to criticize all this incoherence from without: it is frequently condemned from within and its crumbling fissures are openly confessed.

The Church from Below Model

Although it is often unclear who is ordained or not in an HTB church, there is an Anglican priest in charge because they ostensibly work through the parish system, even if they do not act parochially. They rely on the parish system to operate and expand, yet treat it parasitically, like a new cuckoo denouncing the nest of the past yet continuing to depend upon its nesting within it. It is this hybridity that ensures the model of planting is really one of transplanting coordinated from above.

By contrast, many of the pioneers who start completely new churches or work towards them in the 'new worshipping communities' arm of the mixed economy/ecology, are not clergy as in the church planting model but lay evangelists. But the problem they experience with church structures and authority lies in the fact that this work aims to be a different mode of church planting, albeit from below, *rather than* evangelism pure and simple. Myriad supports both modes of planting.

Such pioneers undertake an impressive range of community support projects, based on careful attention to local needs, from children's clothes swaps to community gardening or debt advice. There are community cafes, food banks and all sorts of good things happening, just as in parish churches. But instead of integrating the worshipping community they engender into the local church, so that the group might have their own prayer or fellowship group, yet also join with the main worshipping community in the parish church, they insist on being an independent church plant, without accepting the orders and structure of Anglican polity. The added value to the parish of evangelistic outreach is foregone in favour of the establishing of the rival speculative value of competitive institutional groupings.

Thus, we have a situation in which one lay leader is reported as not knowing what the diocese even was, while others rejected invitations to become Readers or to join the ordained ministry.[14] That is fine if these people want to be evangelists out on the edge, where they can indeed be entrepreneurial and independent, but to resist the presence of the priest, or have anything to do with the parish church – on the grounds that if the people they have gathered had wanted to be part of it they would have gone there, as one lay-leader suggests in the report – is neither long-term sustainable nor authentically Anglican.[15] It renders the new worshipping community highly vulnerable if the leader moves on, since it is so centred on the personality of the evangelist. Links to an established, stable parochial community would be a countervailing strength and enable continuity at times of change.

The most extensive research on these new plants is George Lings' four-year study of Fresh Expressions for the Church Army, *Encountering the Day of Small Things*, published in 2017. The report is anxious to claim that the new worshipping communities are churches and is critical of the earlier Anglican/Methodist report *Fresh Expressions in the Mission of the Church* (2012) for its eight marks of what makes a church, which Lings considers too strict. In particular, he questions the practice-based model, meaning a church is partly defined as a community where baptisms and Holy Communion take place.

> The practice-based approach is significantly prejudicial against young churches whose identity lies deeper than their performance, and whose identity is more closely connected to their intentions and potential. The same critique would be true in arguing against any thinking that children are not fully human, because they are not yet adults with attendant possessions, employment, earning power or social patterns, let alone the elusive quality of maturity.[16]

The analogy does not hold, because with a baby there is no question that he or she grows up as a human being, but all sorts of different future scenarios are possible for the future of an under-five meeting, a skateboarding Fresh Expression or Bible-study group. Growth towards the commitment of Baptism will demonstrate whether it has the potential to become a church. Up to that point it is a form of missional or catechetical outreach.

Furthermore, as so much twentieth-century theology has made us aware, it is the Eucharist that makes the church. To be Christian *is* to be a sharer in the body of Christ through baptism and communion. Even at the highpoint of Reformation Protestantism, Article 19 of the Thirty-Nine Articles states that 'the visible Church of Christ is a congregation of faithful men, in which the pure Word of God is preached, and the Sacraments be duly ministered according to Christ's ordinance'.[17] Yet among the new worshipping communities in twenty-one dioceses, over a four-year period, only 46% had celebrated Holy Communion, 42.1% had held a baptism and 30.3% had held a confirmation – and this figure includes the church plants of HTB style as well as more experimental groups.[18] Again, this figure is not so bad if one considers these as modes of evangelistic outreach, but for independent churches as these claim to be, this is just not right.

Myriad's lay-led churches share certain features with the church-planting model, in that they tend to assume they are planting into inert soil. Unlike HTB however, which tends to make use of church buildings, these meet in cafes or homes and have a rather different vision. In some ways the ecclesiology is an attractive and important one, which often involves living alongside the people whom the pioneers are evangelizing, such as Steve and Gift who in 2020 lived on the Nook Farm Syke estate in Rochdale: 'our hope is to truly become part of this community and share Jesus with the people we meet in the rhythms of everyday life on the estate'.[19] Such ministry is wholly Anglican in inspiration and incarnational in its theology.

Rochdale, however, our Anglican Happy Valley, reveals some of the ironies in the whole mixed ecology approach, in that millions are spent to create and endow Nelson Street Resource Church, just a three-minute walk from the parish church, when this money could have been used to establish a church and community centre on Steve and Gift's Syke estate, one and a half miles to the north, where there is none; it could have been a sign to those people of their worth and value. Perhaps church planters here would reply like those who withdrew from a plant in one of Nottinghamshire's most deprived towns, respond: 'it's not our demographic'. It seems that an ecclesiology from below is for the working-classes, and the post-industrial heartlands, with HTB church for the more affluent suburban hubs – though both of them are unlike the church for everyone embodied by the parish idea. The parish church in Rochdale is literally and ecclesiologically caught between the two.

In contrast to the HTB model, where a social service might be started almost immediately, the Myriad mode of planting tries to work from below and often thinks long and hard before moving into action. The Church of England defines pioneer ministry in this way: 'Pioneers are people called by God who are the first to see and creatively respond to the Holy Spirit's initiatives with those outside the church; gathering others around them as they seek to establish new contextual Christian community.'[20]

This view of the Church is quite close to that of liberal 1960s South Bank theology in that it emphasizes the work of the Holy Spirit in all acts of goodness, hospitality and justice. It also echoes something of that religionless Christianity in that it suggests a separate mission from that of the Church in the reference to 'the Holy Spirit's initiatives'. Frequently, one reads of pioneers finding out what the Holy Spirit is doing and joining in: as if she were a mythical deity operating in independence from the other persons of the Trinity and not the Spirit of the Son, who is the concretely expressed and revealed Word of the Father. The aim is to get people to understand the implicit Christianity in what they are doing and to learn to articulate it through worship. Lings' report states that in some cases leaders have not 'forced our initiative to be a fresh expression of church from the start' but instead 'have deliberately left time and space for the group to evolve and "own" its ecclesial identity'.[21]

These pioneers or planters are of course right to see the Holy Spirit at work everywhere and to help nurture people of good will and projects that serve the kingdom. Understanding that all believers are doing theology in their actions is also important. Equally so is the contextual nature of this reflection in which, if our theology is real, it will have something to say to the particular situation in which we live and work.

The ecclesiological outworking of all this in these projects, however, can sometimes be in the direction of the local group *inventing* the religious expression this takes. Indeed, I have heard proponents of contextual theology opine that we should not impose liturgy, belief or doctrine upon these groups. This may be one reason why the sacraments are not the goal or practice of these communities, in that they wait patiently for faith and worship to emerge from the context, as if that context were impossibly free-floating in relation to human history and wider community. They forget that worship is not simply something that we do but is also a gift from God, which is why the angels are so important in liturgy, as we learn to model their spontaneous heavenly adoration.

In order to become sacramental communities, lay-led Fresh Expressions (which is now interchangeable with 'new worshipping community') will have to develop some form of connection to the wider church in a relation with their local parish priest. By contrast, Lings notes 63 Fresh Expressions in which Holy Communion is irregularly and illegally lay-led. This figure does include some agape meals and eight usages of communion by extension, but there are a remaining 31 worshipping communities where the Communion is always lay-led, which goes clean against Anglican ecclesiology and the legacy of Christian orthodox practice.[22] Lings claims that a lay-presidency revolt is 'far-fetched' but it seems to be already a reality in some places. Again, money and resources are being given to projects that are not Anglican in polity or sacramental expression and to split approaches that consciously uphold an educational and material class-divide, again in total contrast to all the official rhetoric.

Ideally, the new worshipping community would become

one of the parish's congregations, unless it is geographically discrete, as on a particular new estate, and numerically large enough to become its own parish, as was the practice in earlier periods of urban evangelism. It is ironic that, despite all the claims of *Mission-Shaped Church* that we are now a network culture, and so evangelism should abandon the geographic for the homogenous unit principle, most Fresh Expressions, according to Lings' research, are locally based, with 71% of attendees coming from the immediate area.[23] Like HTB style transplants, which seem to exist just to reproduce further identical and semi-detached cells, it seems that the other forms of new worshipping community similarly have little vision of how they might be connected to the wider church.

One particularly bizarre example is the Leesland Neighbourhood Church in Gosport, Hampshire. It was closed as St Faith's parish church because the congregation was too small, but then promptly financed to open as a new worshipping community, with staff running toddler groups, Hallowe'en light festivities and other activities that are standard fare of good parochial ministry.[24] What was the point of stopping it being a parish church? The answer seems to be ideological. Moreover, having spent money setting it up, the diocese then adds a further level of incoherence: 'As part of the diocese's pastoral reorganization, another church nearby (300–500 metres away) is now partnering with Harbour Church and accessing funding that will enable them to put on events "way beyond anything we could ever resource or afford to do" and which may be hard to compete with.'[25]

Of course, it is important to remember how many Fresh Expressions are, in reality, modes of existing parish outreach. Messy Church in the Church Army report accounted for 32% of all Fresh Expressions and these are parish initiatives. Indeed, Messy Church originates not from HTB but from the Bible Reading Fellowship. However, most Messy Churches do not have sacramental worship: 12.8% had held a Communion service, 21.7% a baptism and 10.2% a confirmation. This is less worrying when they are an evangelistic outreach by a parish, which already offers the sacraments, but it is still revealing of contorted priorities, if the Messy Church is to be a church as such, and not one manifestation of a parish church's worship.

Messy Church is a nonetheless excellent programme that, like the Alpha Course, has instant brand recognition. It too has a hospitality element with food provided, though there is sometimes a small fee to cover costs. As a mode of outreach that is non-threatening and inclusive it works well, with the craft element uniting parents and children. The worship dimension is naturally focused on children, with songs they can readily join in with. This again is good for an introduction to Christianity and the Bible, but hardly a sustainable diet for an adult over time, if it is to be the main mode of worship and a 'church' rather than a mid-week Sunday School.

I have twice had experience of running similar ventures prior to the Messy Church era and found the parents enjoyed being part of the activity and worship. But in each case, this was not a self-sufficient 'church'. In Lancaster, in a working-class urban parish, the parents often preferred to attend the children's church on Sundays and to join the main service for communion. In this way, the adults could put their toe into the waters of public worship. Likewise, in a Nottinghamshire village the mid-week session, attended by parents and children, always prepared some drama or artwork for the monthly parish family eucharist. Even today, in one South Gloucestershire village, the successful Messy Church precedes the main service like a conventional Children's Church.

In order to make Messy Church more sustaining as a main mode of adult formation, you would need to separate parents and children for distinct teaching sessions and widen and deepen the worshipping element. It might involve all contributing to one larger artwork and moving away from the individual choice of the order in which one attempts particular activities, so as to become more liturgical and gathered. The Messy Church website includes ideas for a Messy Baptism and parishes such as St Nicholas Abbots Bromley celebrate Holy Communion as well as Messy Baptism with richly symbolic crafts:

The church was packed and activities included candle cakes, marbling, paper chains, water pistols extinguishing candles and prayers on doves which 'flew' in church for quite a while afterwards. All the activities linked closely to the Baptism Service.[26]

There is potential then in Messy Church and the more recent Wild or Forest Church to be a true congregation, especially when, as in Abbots Bromley, the worship is structured to include the key elements of Anglican liturgy.

The parochial model, when well done, combines the best of the two novel ecclesial modes I have discussed, but also includes elements that they leave out. The parish church building, a key missional element, is included in the church transplant model, but its cure of souls to the whole parish through life-events ministry is neglected and its worship eviscerated. The new worship community shares its parochial commitment to the whole local area but not its sacramental worship or interdependence or shared ministry. Far too often it simply ignores Anglican tradition and defines itself against it. Lings goes so far as to write caustically about 'so-called churches': 'if the Spirit of God should take an extended sabbatical then absolutely nothing would change as a result'.[27] He questions whether some parish churches are really 'church' at all. This is arrogantly to scorn the lives and witness of far too many, including many saints.

There is much for those in parish ministry to learn from the positivity and hospitality of the HTB model, and from the contextual embeddedness of pioneer ministry. A more truly ecological and organic missional vision would focus, however, on the core parochial model and not sacrifice it to these ecclesial idols, which is what they have become in the panic to grow the Church in a time of mounting secularism and atheism. It would find a way to strengthen the relation between parish and mission initiative and call the planting model back to something more Anglican. We need to be one ecclesial body once again.

6

Bishops and Parishes:
What is the Church?

What is the Local Church?

If you ask many ordinary churchgoers the name of their diocese, they are often unsure, as it does not feature much in their
lives. The bishop may be encountered at a confirmation service
and the cathedral visited on occasion, but the diocese itself as
an entity does not really intrude, unless they are members of
a PCC and then it becomes the bureaucratic body that orders
them to have a quinquennial inspection or sends forms that
need to be completed.

And yet, if you ask an ecclesiologist, you will be told that the
diocese is the true local church and not the parish.

The model being followed is that of the Canon Law of the
Roman Catholic Church, where a diocese is defined as follows:

A portion of the people of God which is entrusted to a bishop
for him to shepherd with the cooperation of the presbyterium,
so that, adhering to its pastor and gathered by him in the Holy
Spirit through the gospel and the Eucharist, it constitutes a
particular church in which the one, holy, catholic Church of
Christ is truly present and operative.[1]

Anglicans too are episcopalian and so we can agree with this
idea that the fullness of the Church is shown when the people
and clergy are gathered with their bishop. Paul Avis, in his
Identity of Anglicanism, similarly defines the local church in
this way:

In Anglicanism, the diocese, as the community united in its bishop and as the bishop's sphere of ministry, is regarded ecclesiologically as the 'local church'. It is the *locus* or sphere of the bishop's oversight and of the bishop's collegial ministry with the presbyterate, assisted by the deacons, in every place.[2]

St Ignatius at the end of the first century puts it more poetically:

> For your justly renowned presbytery, worthy of God, is fitted as exactly to the bishop as the strings are to a harp. Therefore in your concord and harmonious love, Jesus Christ is sung. And do ye, man by man, become a choir, that being harmonious in love, and taking up the song of God in unison, ye may with one voice sing to the Father through Jesus Christ.[3]

Paul Avis's and Ignatius's statements, despite stressing the focus on the bishop, whose sway extends beyond the immediately local, also however emphasize the interdependence and relationality of church structure, stretching down to the most intimate level, which is a glorious symbol of the unity of the Godhead itself, as well as the variety and splendour of the creation. Ignatius is famous for his advocacy of the episcopal office and yet he understands it as nested within the presbyterium and the laity as singing to its music, or perhaps as the notes themselves. Every element here has its part to play, from the laity to their bishop, from the most local to the more extensive.

Richard Hooker is instructive here. Writing to defend the practice of episcopacy against the Puritans and Presbyterians, he nonetheless defines the nature of episcopacy quite narrowly. A bishop is defined as:

> A minister of God, unto whom with permanent continuance, there is given not only power of administering the Word and Sacraments, which power other Presbyters have; but also a further power to ordain Ecclesiastical persons, and a power of Chiefty in government over Presbyters as well as Lay men, a power to be by way of jurisdiction a Pastor even to Pastors themselves.[4]

The territorial or 'diocesan' aspect develops over time, but it is the power to ordain, not territorial oversight, which distinguishes the episcopal role and his pastoral oversight over clergy and people.

There is in all three of these extracts an emphasis on participated authority operating through the priesthood/presbyterate, which is represented in the parish setting by the priest holding the cure of souls on behalf of the bishop, while the harmony of the congregation arises in relation to the reflected unity of the bishop him or herself. The word 'diocese' does not appear either in Hooker or Ignatius. Diocese could not appear in Ignatius, because it did not then exist, being a late Roman administrative term for a section of a province.[5] This became adapted to describe a bishop's court and was revived as an idea by Emperor Charlemagne in the late eighth century as part of his classicizing agenda, to make his rule seem like that of a new Rome. It became a term to describe the territorial limits of the see of a bishop and so it has continued. Even Hooker just writes of the restraint of 'some definite, local compass' in which the regiment of the bishop may be exercised.[6]

Defending the Parish as Key Element in Church Structure

This does not mean that the parish, 'the most local level of the Church' as Avis describes it, has no anciently dispersed authority or ecclesial meaning, as too many rather amateur ecclesiologists would attempt to persuade us. This was the view put forward by Siôn Rhys Evans in a *Church Times* webinar on whether the parish needs saving. Angela Tilby reported a remark in a leaving sermon by the retiring Bishop of Portsmouth, Christopher Foster, as saying, perhaps despairingly, that we should now regard the diocese as the parish.[7] Indeed, as the geographical parish, which is how it is first recognized ecclesiologically, the parish is the basis alongside the adjacent parishes for the eventual *emergence* of the diocese. So, the diocese is not in essence a controlling bureaucracy but is rather a kind of 'parish of parishes', held in unity with the bishop through the sharing of the cure of souls with the incumbent.[8] Without the geographical parishes, there would be no diocese: in its origin the latter term denotes the oversight of those units by the bishop. Indeed, the term *paroikia* predates that of diocese by several centuries, as the 'beside the house' or sojourning place, where clergy ministered to those in the countryside.[9]

What is happening in recent Anglican episcopal practice is an attempt to use the legal language of the diocese as the most local level of the church in order to remove the participation of the parish and with it all real and genuine localism. Some dioceses follow Catholic practice and define themselves as 'the household of faith', which is true in the same way that the whole Church is one family: the word 'ecumenical' is derived from *oikos,* meaning 'house' in Greek. Yet every level of ecclesial belonging is in this sense a household, beginning with the actual family and moving outwards to the parish, deanery, diocese and beyond. The problem is that in making so much of the diocese as the 'primary local church' the parish is no longer regarded as a devolved symbol of ecclesial unity and *koinonia* at the local level but a mere assembly, which can be easily removed because the basic unit is taken to be the (in practice much more abstract and remote) diocese on more than questionable historical and theological foundations.

Formerly, in the parish system, which is universal among ancient churches and not just an Anglican mode of organization, the diocese *was* indeed the union of parishes and people under the bishop. But today that element of hierarchical participation of structures and clergy is being removed, especially through the way in which the cure of souls is being treated. Huge mega-benefices are being created with vestigial pastoral care and liturgical provision, despite Canon C18 of the Anglican Canon Law, which states that 'in every place within his diocese there shall be sufficient priests to minister the word and sacrament to the people that are therein'.[10] Place is now being stretched to encompass areas that no one locally would think of as a single 'place' at all.

Canon 18 also defines a bishop's role as one of chief pastor to clergy and laity alike, teacher and upholder of doctrine, keeper of peace and order and holder of jurisdiction. In these roles are summed up the two poles of unity that the bishop traditionally embodies: unity of structure and unity of faith, about which Cyprian of Carthage wrote so eloquently in the third century:

> The Church also is one, which is spread abroad far and wide into a multitude by an increase of fruitfulness. As there are many rays of the sun, but one light; and many branches of a tree, but one strength based on its tenacious root; and since from one spring flow many streams, and though the multiplicity seems diffused in the liberality of an overflowing abundance, yet the unity is preserved in one source ... It is the same with the Church... Her fruitful abundance spreads her branches over the whole world. She broadly expands her rivers, liberally flowing, yet her head is one, and she is one mother, plentiful in the results of fruitfulness. From her womb we are born, by her milk we are nourished, by her spirit we are animated.[11]

By this analogy, the bishop is the branch here, as part of the tree, and the parishes are twigs held by the branch, which is itself in connection to the root, which is Christ himself. Or in his watery metaphor, parishes are the little rivulets from the stream, which is fed from the river. Note that Cyprian's arboreal image honours every level of the Church's fruitfulness, from the local and even individual to the stem. Moreover, in tree growth life comes from the twigs.

The tendency in contemporary Anglican policy is to dishonour and collapse the different levels or arboreal elements in a move to centralization, increasing diocesan bureaucracies and the power of the bishop. Anecdotally, I am told that some bishops are frustrated by the limits of their authority and command. This can only be because their idea of their role has lost its pastoral and teaching heart and become one akin to a CEO of a business. But dioceses are not at all like businesses and this desire will always be frustrated.

Loss of Role of Area or Rural Dean as Advocate of Clergy and Parishes

It is not just the parish that loses its identity in this drive to collapse structures: the dual role of the rural or area dean has also been lost. The position has evolved over the years and has historically been a conduit between the bishop and his clergy, as these words from Samuel Wilberforce demonstrate:

> My great object is that the Rural Dean should form an easy and accurate medium of communication between me and the clergy of the Deanery, and still more that he should be a local centre of spiritual influence and brotherly union to his clergy: being himself a pattern of the true Spiritual Pastor's life, leading all around him into more zeal and more unity.[12]

The rural or area dean was a first among equals of the local clergy and in some cases (such as Exeter and Truro) was elected by them, though annual elections proved impractical, and bishops took the appointment of rural deans into their own hands during the nineteenth century, when the office became more significant as diocesan structures grew in importance.[13] There is some evidence, however, that in the West Country, election of rural deans was a practice as late as the 1990s. Notably, the *Handbook for Area Deans* in Exeter Diocese has a strong theology of the role:

> They exercise a *diaconal* ministry of service to their colleagues, ordained and lay, being attentive as far as possible to their needs and concerns and seeking to address them. As *priests* they exercise a ministry of pastoral care, intercession and reconciliation within the Deanery, through which the priesthood of all believers is nourished and strengthened. As Bishop's officers, they share in his/her *episcope*, offering oversight, encouragement, support, vision and sometimes challenge to the churches in their Deanery.[14]

This is exemplary in linking this ministry to the three orders and carefully calibrating the different roles in ways that must, I imagine, be practically helpful as well as ecclesiologically rich. And still today this element of clerical representation remains in the Diocese of London's *Handbook for Area Deans*, which states, 'It is important to remember that the Area Dean is both a bishop's officer and a parish priest, with a role as advocate on behalf of the clergy, a communication link between the bishop and the parishes and in a position to represent the needs and thinking of the clergy to the bishop.' The handbook emphasizes that the Dean is not an Archdeacon's assistant. Described as the bishop's spectacles and also as a kind of trade union representative for the clergy, the area dean is part of the dispersed authority structure of a dynamic dispositive hierarchy, which honours the lowest level of organization.

In recent years however, the rural dean's role in relation to the bishop and diocesan structure has been much more emphasized and that of the clergy and parishes' advocate downplayed. In part this is once more to do with the imposition of management models on the Church, where a command-and-control single line of authority puts the Dean under the Archdeacon and adds greatly to the administrative burden of the role.[15] This is then reflected in the increasing tendency to decouple such roles from any parish ministry, thereby at a stroke severing the Dean from the lived experience of those he or she represents.

Employed by the diocese, the Dean then sees him or herself as primarily an employee, with responsibilities mainly oriented upward. When one examines the job descriptions of such roles, they tend towards pastoral reorganization, of which area deans are the local enforcers, as well as missional strategy.

In the examples I have looked at, however, missional language of strategy always plays out in the direction of getting the parishes to agree to new mergers and sharing of clergy. In Chelmsford, the Area Dean is openly renamed: 'Rural Missioner'. No wonder parishes find the deanery an odd structure. Its former role was as a clerical chapter under the dean (which goes back over a thousand years), with oversight of his clergy in treating buildings and contents properly and performing their role of cure of souls effectively. Now its function seems mainly to bring parishes together in order ultimately to merge them.

There are obvious benefits in the deanery structure for small parishes and certain tasks and purchases can be done better communally. Yet the primary unit is the parish, with the priest its main link to the deanery through the rural or area dean. Effective pastoral care happens within the network of local relations and associations, where need can be discerned through the parishioners themselves. Taxi-rank operations through a deanery office are far less practical or successful. Moreover, the merging of churches forces people to travel extensively (if they are able to do so) in order to find worship to attend or pastors to call on.

Bishops' Power and Bishops' Mission Orders

So great is the turn from pastoral care and teaching (leaving the field free to secular 'therapy') to managerial mission in the Church of England, that recent discussion describes bishops rather as 'brokers in mission', employing again the language of the stock exchange and doing so in the context of the development of Bishops' Mission Orders that have allowed bishops to ride roughshod over parochial boundaries and authority. Section 4.3.3 of a Bishop's Mission Order allows the bishop to overrule the authority of the incumbent as holder of the cure of souls, which would normally allow him or her to decide who might minister, teach or preach in the parish. The Bishop of Manchester has put the whole diocese under a BMO, which means he may do more or less what he likes.[16] Again, this is to collapse the discrete layers of shared *episcope* hitherto in operation and to disempower the parish church. It is to operate on the command-and-control method of old-fashioned managerialism, characteristic of the 1980s, which has been widely criticized.

If this top-down managerial style is used to quash the independence and autonomy of priest and parish, it is also used to secure the same for the new worshipping community or fresh expression, in relation to its parish rival. Where command-and-control is, to some extent, necessary is in the armed forces on the battlefield, but there it works to ensure the organic interdependence of each unit, so that they work together effect-ively, like a tree or a river-system, to invoke Cyprian. However, like the Church, the armed services are hierarchical, which means the giving of the self to each level below and learning from above. As I have tried to demonstrate, a hierarchy gives due honour to each rank and the virtues it embodies, since it is not ultimately the General who stands on the front-line. Command-and-control in the current Church of England does not, however, honour the levels below but acts unilaterally. It is less subsidiarist than the military and in consequence far less effective.

Even in Ignatius of Antioch's writings, one finds a view of episcopacy as collaborative. The bishop does indeed stand for Christ, and one should do nothing without him, but this is equally true of the priesthood. Bishop and presbyterium are frequently spoken of in one phrase in Ignatius and the latter are also given authority:

> It is therefore necessary that, as ye indeed do, so without the bishop ye should do nothing, but should also be subject to the presbytery, as to the apostle of Jesus Christ, who is our hope, in whom, if we live, we shall [at last] be found.[17]

Bishops and Archbishops

Bishops in the contemporary Church of England, however, have precious little time to sit with their clergy. A number of them sit in the House of Lords and carry a quasi-ministerial brief, on which they feel the need to opine on all suitable occasions, thereby perhaps encouraging their imminent removal from that august chamber forever. All bishops belong to the College of Bishops and meet twice yearly; diocesan bishops and a number of elected suffragans and some others meet as the House of Bishops, also biannually. The House of Bishops additionally sit in General Synod, while a couple sit on the Archbishops' Coun-cil. There are also sub-committees. Bishop's Council is the main consultative body in a diocese; it has lay representation but little in the way of ordinary clergy, just a sprinkling of officeholders.

And while some bishops may unrealistically bewail their inability to do exactly what they would like within their diocese, they do seem to have far less independence than formerly in relation to the Archbishops. Where once the role of the metropolitan was to keep the peace, they now receive an oath of obedience from the other bishops in their province, who promise their archbishop 'all due reverence and obedience'.[18]

Priests and deacons make a similar oath to their bishop but with one key difference: they pay 'true and canonical obedience to the Lord Bishop of C and his successors in all things lawful and honest'.[19] Formerly, bishops paid 'due allegiance', which is a more feudal relation but a relational oath nonetheless, and which is about loyalty and trust. It seems that they are now to give obedience but without any caveat still allowed to the lower clergy of obeying only in matters 'lawful and honest'.[20] In practice, one has the impression as an outsider that the bishops increasingly operate according to a party line and feel beholden to do so.

Ever since 1998, moreover, there has been the Archbishops' Council, which is mainly made up of appointees and which enables the archbishops to wield enormous power. In the proposals put forward in the recent Governance Review, the role of the Church Commissioners will be lessened in scope, and power will be concentrated even more centrally within the new body, CENS, Church of England National Services.[21] The Governance Review Report deliberately downgrades the role of the House of Bishops, which is chided for daring to publish some pastoral guidelines for dealing with same-sex marriages, even though that seemed, given its pastoral remit, wholly appropriate for the time being, given that no new arrangements or policy had been decided at the General Synod. Indeed, paragraph 98 is particularly chilling in regard to the role of the bishop:

> The GRG has also observed that the fact that bishops are so strongly identified with location potentially makes it more difficult for them to come to a collective, national view and/or be loyal to decisions taken in the national interest. Indeed, some have suggested that the nature of the episcopal appointment

process may not produce the candidates best equipped for visionary national leadership if such candidates are chosen based on local needs rather than the broader make-up of the House of Bishops.[22]

Although an alternative view of the specificity of the bishop's location is also presented, the official view is that this gets in the way of a specifically national and so very 'political' sounding body, to which one might well ask: do we need this? STP has often observed that tasks such as safeguarding could more effectively be administered centrally and that diocesan managerial structures should be severely pruned, but that is to bring bishops closer to their flocks and render episcopal ministry more locally focused, not less. As in Parliament, local knowledge and commitment is essential. Suggesting that local and national ecclesial decisions would be at odds is strange, given the inherently devolved nature of the diocese and its duty to reflect the local upwards.

Just as a diocese is a 'parish of parishes', so also a province is a 'diocese of dioceses' and the national English church is co-provincial. This echoes the way in which traditionally a polity was seen as a 'community of communities' before it was replaced by the modern liberal notion of a 'state' exercising monopolized central power over a population of otherwise disconnected individuals. But Anglican thinkers in the tradition of Hooker have often criticized this Hobbesian and Lockean model and right into the twentieth century, theologians like John Neville Figgis supported an alternative pluralist and dispersed model of sovereignty, linked to a nested organicism of communities. Today all this legacy is abandoned, if it is even recalled: archiepiscopacy itself is thought of as operating on a detached and independent 'state' model, ironically rather like that of the modern Catholic papacy whose absolutism was itself an initial model for the emergence of the national 'state'.[23]

No examples of possible conflicts between local and national are, however, actually suggested in the report and I think what lies behind it is rather the desire of the present archbishops to have Vision and Strategy, Emerging Church and their other pet projects driven through the Church of England in the same way everywhere, whereas our current modes of subsidiarist and organic authority just do not allow this. So, the brave Bishop of Chelmsford, the Revd Dr Giuli Francis-Dehqani, was reported in the *Church Times* as telling her Diocesan Synod that 'the language of vision and strategy risks ignoring the reality of frailty, brokenness, sin' and that 'everyone following the same programme is not the only way'.[24] She later informed her synod that the traditional top-down approach would be 'tipped on its head. There will be no more initiatives imposed from the so-called centre', but instead a focus on local discernment and discovery.[25] She is right: working out with parishes in the local diocese particular priorities and plans is much more likely to be effective. If parishes are ignored, or used as pawns in grand merger schemes, it is improbable that members of their congregations will act as the missional disciples recent strategies require them to become.

Governance Review and Centralized Power

There are some dioceses quietly going about their key work without undue mergers and grand strategies, but it seems that the Governance Review seeks to standardize diocesan strategy. In the reforms proposed there would be a college of all 112 bishops, directed by a Board of twelve Bishops, out of whom a few would serve on the CENS (Church of England National Services). In the first option of CENS membership there would be just two in a mix that would allow appointees to outnumber elected members. Option 2 would allow four bishops and four Synod members, of whom no more than two could be clergy, plus six extra lay appointees, while Option 3 suggests some open process of application.[26] In an amendment, the July 2023 General Synod did manage to direct that more than half the members of CENS should be elected or appointed by Synod.

Lower clergy are sparsely represented in all of the three options, which is particularly unfortunate, given the proposal that the oversight of Mission and Pastoral Measures and of potential appeals against them, which will involve church closures and impact clergy and parishes, is to be transferred across to the central committee from the Church Commissioners. The latter will additionally lose the Mission, Pastoral and Property Committee and Church Buildings Council, which will also be transferred. Paragraph 180 stresses 'while we do not consider that these functions need to be independently governed, we do underline the need for appellate functions to be carried out objectively', but how this could be achieved is opaque, given that church closures are very much part of top-down diocesan strategy led by the Archbishops' Council's Strategic Transformation Fund.[27] There is a crying need for some kind of independent ombudsman role, given the downgrading of the role of the Church Commissioners, or even better, that the appellate functions be preserved and strengthened, with the independence that the Pensions Board enjoys.

This CENS committee will therefore be enormously powerful; it intends to devise national strategy and downgrade the role of dioceses in making their own decisions, specific to context, let alone allowing parishes to have some level of self-determination. So, despite the false claims made for the priority of the diocese, it turns out that the diocese needs saving as well as the parish.

It is noticeable how the Review Group behind the report are also impatient about the power of General Synod to approve legislation and doubt that it has the capacity to do this work, wishing to reserve more to the central committee. I quoted Martyn Percy earlier, who made analogies with the Chinese Communist Party, but the centralizing agenda is certainly a feature common to China and the Church of England. One might reasonably argue that the various central bodies in the Church of England are complicated, and could be streamlined and simplified, but how the Lambeth and Bishopsthorpe operations conform to such a goal here is not addressed. Rather, they appear to be a way of clawing as much power as possible to CENS, while depriving the Church Commissioners of their appellate function, General Synod of its legislative role and the House of Bishops (which consists of diocesans with some suffragan representation) of any role whatsoever.

The new Board of Bishops would presumably contain the other new role, which is a development of the lead bishop, often linked to House of Lords responsibilities. This is the cabinet minister idea, which has been mooted in a Consultation Document, *Bishops and Ministry Fit for a New Context*, and which divorces some bishops from any diocesan role at all, but makes them Bishop for Brexit, Levelling-up or the Environment and so forth. Papal curia appointments are somewhat of this nature but are at least made for a global church, not a merely national body.

Martyn Percy's interpretation of this document regards it as a move still further from the local:

If power and authority shifts from the ground (spatial) to the situational and subject-based, the net result will be inherently non-local and anti-democratic. The business of representation – whether accountable or symbolic – will shift to arenas where Bishops have designated responsibility and opinions. Or perhaps Bishops may go further and claim vicarious expertise on behalf of the church and its collective members.[28]

I am not an ecclesial organizational expert and feel often quite overwhelmed by the numbers of reports and consultation documents the Church of England generates. It is a very wordy body and seems to relish committees. The Church should do less self-examination, opine less frequently and allow each level of its various ecclesial manifestations to attend to its core activities and enjoy its own dignity.

Enabling Each Level: the Virtuous Hierarchy

It is common for people to speak in derogative terms about hierarchies, but they are central to the Christian Neo-Platonism which has come down to us from the Patristic and Medieval theological tradition, beginning with St Paul himself. A virtuous hierarchy is the opposite of command-and-control, in that every level assists and exalts the one below.[29] A genuine hierarchy is also combined with equality in that God creates and relates to each one of us equally but according to our capacity. There is a hierarchy in the operation of Christian virtue insofar as love or charity raises each of us up to our *telos* or goal of union with God. Aquinas calls love the form of the virtues because it directs and shapes them so that they are oriented to the ultimate.

In the same way, the bishop should enable each person, each parish, each deanery to flourish as fully as it can and to fulfil its purpose. Colin Podmore locates the *episcope* of the bishop precisely as relational, relating local to universal and enabling every level to flourish.[30] Levels and modes of activity are clearly related, and each step of the hierarchical ladder must be acknowledged, for hierarchy fails in its purpose when they are muddled or subsumed. A family is an obvious example. Parents need to assume responsibility, but the aim of parenthood is to raise children who will be independent and flourish, forming their own families. Be too much like a friend rather than a parent and you deny your child the care and discipline that he or she needs to grow morally. On the other hand, not treating children respectfully will equally stunt their development. The writer of Colossians invokes a parental or pedagogical analogy for the role of the apostle in relation to those under his care: 'It is he whom we proclaim, warning everyone and teaching everyone in all wisdom, so that we may present everyone mature in Christ' (Col. 1.38).

But a muddling and subsumption of hierarchical levels is what characterizes the Church of England at present. Supposed financial pressures have reduced the numbers of clergy available and, instead, lay people are being asked to step into their role. Mission hubs wish to create 'focal ministers' who will act as pastor and leader for a local church, while the clergy act only centrally. This is presented as honouring the ministry of the laity, but as I argued in previous chapters, it is instead obscuring the true vocation of being lay. In the Reformation, where the vocation of being a lay person began to be more developed (often in a perfectly 'Catholic' fashion), it was in relation to one's calling by God to a trade and to family life. The worlds of work and the household were now to be seen as sacred arenas where the gospel could be lived out. Luther's understanding of vocation is well summarized by Hart:

The life God wants most people to lead is the life of daily work, and therefore such a life is holy and sacred and fully pleasing to God – in no way of less value in God's eyes than a life spent in prayer or church work. His other important thrusts were that each person should regard their job as a calling and stay in it; that menial work is of equal value to work more highly regarded by men; that one's work must serve one's ... neighbour; and his concern for honesty and fair dealing in one's work.[31]

While retired people are those often in the sights of those who seek focal ministers, and generally, civil society is kept going by this group, this is not necessarily the case. With respect to those of working age, the Church is taking people away from or diluting their primary calling to be a minister, and is therefore, if they are not to be ordained, downgrading both the role of cure of souls on the one hand and the lay vocation on the other.

A whole parallel system of licensed lay ministry is growing up which has little to do with lay work and everything to do with a kind of sub-diaconate or priesthood, though without an ecclesial understanding of how it fits with the threefold ministry. The role of a Reader was openly a form of this, with its own specific training for readiness to lead services of the Word and preach. It developed the ancient role of Lector, which Elizabeth I revived in the Anglican Church in 1565 to enable Epistle reading in collegiate and cathedral churches. In 1866 it was again revived as Reader ministry, with preaching added. This role was inherently liturgical, but has now been mirrored, and in most dioceses replaced, by LLMs or Licensed Lay Ministry, which is much wider and vaguer. In the St Mellitus BA in Theology, Ministry and Mission, components of which are taken by LLMs, there is no compulsory study of liturgy.[32] Sarum College, which has a rich variety of courses, offers, I believe, only a practical weekend on 'how to do a funeral' and other liturgical tasks – and that is for ordinands. How anyone could be a focal minister without some understanding of liturgy is beyond me.

Even the role of pastoral care is quite differently exercised by an ordained minister from a lay visitor. The latter is one of the community-visiting of a fellow parishioner on behalf of the local Church. The former visits both as the local pastor and representative of the whole Church, mediating the bishop's own pastoral care and oversight and able to offer communion. The distance from the most local immediacy of the priest or deacon is central to the performance of cure of souls. Locally superb mutual care is offered by parishioners to each other, and some lay people may have better skills in this area than their vicar. But the ministry of the cure of souls is distinct. It is the shared episcope of the priest which involves a sense of distance, essential to pastoral ministry in a role which is both local and also linked to the wider church that makes the difference, as well as the way in which the pastoral visit could develop sacramentally, whether into Holy Communion, Unction or Reconciliation.

The Anglican ethicist Oliver O'Donovan has a helpful discussion of the nature of episcopal authority in his Bampton Lectures, *The Ways of Judgement*. There he derives a ministry of teaching from the development of the episcopate from the original authority of the apostles as those who had seen Christ:

> The function of the increasingly devolved responsibility was to secure the normativity of the apostolic Gospel for each place, mediating between the universality of the word and the contingency of localities. It was to defend the effectiveness of the new communities that the preaching of the Gospel established, to defend the integrity of the local church as a community living in the truth.
>
> The order of responsibility which came to be known as the 'presbyterate', then was charged with protecting the evangelical discourse in the local church.[33]

This means that the parish priest mediates the universality and truth of the gospel and ensures that it is effectively supreme in the local church. The union with the universal Church is also asserted and this is also referred at once upwards through the bishop and downwards to his or her parishioners:

An ecclesial ministry constituted locally must have two aspects, bounded and horizoned, one turned inward, the other outward, one focused on the integrity of *koinonia* within the place, the other on the integrity of *koinonia* with the universal church. The authenticity of the church's local witness to the truth must be protected from two sides, against a deracinated failure to relate it to the actual conditions of the place, and against a parochial isolation and immured self-sufficiency.[34]

Through the ordained minister, this double role can be mediated and the inwardness of too parochial a perspective balanced by universal resonance.

A Way Forward

This chapter, therefore, has argued that we should acknowledge the dignity and honour of every level of ecclesial expression and clerical orders and that our understanding of episcopal governance and hierarchical order should be dynamic. How, therefore, can we make reforms that allow this? First, we need to rethink the role of the bishop. Martyn Percy noted as long ago as the Turnbull Report in 1995 that there was a tendency to equate the head of the body of Christ with the bishop rather than Christ.[35] This may equate to the head of a business but the model of leadership in the New Testament, as Percy points out, is one of service and sacrifice. Bishops need to be relieved from some of the endless compliance and bureaucratic demands of their current workload so that they may be more at the service of their people and more truly act as mediators of the universal church to their parishes.

This could be given liturgical expression at the Oils blessing Maundy Thursday service, when the bishop might wash some feet and have his or her feet washed also. Tom O'Loughlin has written powerfully about the transformative effect of mutual foot-washing, which he is seeking to revive as a practice in the Catholic Church.[36] It would also be wonderful for the bishop to hold a monthly open morning, when anyone might come for counsel. In the Coptic Church this is a weekly practice. The bishop sits on his episcopal throne and waits for visitors. In most English dioceses, it would be unthinkable for lay people just to ring up the bishop and arrange a meeting. Indeed, it is often impossible to telephone a bishop directly or even email: one must always go through a PA. In the academic world in which I work, university professors and even vice-chancellors are not so hedged about and think it routine to answer queries from random schoolchildren or the general public as well as students. Bishops need direct communication and face to face meetings with their people.

Bishops should still have large dwellings, big enough for proper hospitality and some allowance to maintain them, but after that there is no reason why any criterion rather than age should attribute a higher salary to them. Nor do they need chauffeurs. A former bishop of Southwell, Sir Edwin Hoskyns, despite his grand title, used to travel around his diocese on public transport. And if politicians are today back on their bikes, then why not bishops? Gaiters would no longer get in the way.

And now that the function of the crown in appointments has been reduced to agreeing to the one name the Church puts forward, there could be a much greater role for the local laity and clergy in the appointment of their bishop. Hooker, for example, believed that such primacy must be mutual and consensual, so let us find new ways in which everyone in a diocese might come together to listen to Bible exposition and preaching and add the ancient mode of acclamation to the process in some way, so that our bishops' oversight may be truly consensual.

Were the administrative burden reduced, there would be less need for suffragans, which have, like other diocesan officers, grown in number at the same time that parish clergy numbers have been reduced. It would be more satisfying and fulfilling to be a bishop if the number of committees could be reduced and the pastoral and teaching roles could be properly exercised. Decision-making would also become more efficient, because the bishop would then have a much greater knowledge of the diocese and its parishes. Church life with a more available bishop, and archdeacons and area deans with their own parishes would engender a stronger sense of solidarity and communal identity and the cathedral could be used strategically to support this by the presence of the bishop as advisor and make much more sense of invitations to involve the parishes by staging deanery exhibitions, holding diocesan pilgrimages on key saints' days etc.

With the role of the bishop simplified and purified, the roles of archdeacon and rural or area dean will become more attractive, once they are shorn of the role of enforcer of pastoral reorganization and mission strategy. Then, in its turn, the role of the parish priest will itself be returned to a more traditional form and involve less sitting in an office directing others.

This is not to say that an effective incumbent will not be empowering of his or her parishioners and skilled in using the gifts and talents of lay people, but that this will come from working with them rather than from a managerial distance. So, one of the priests I studied as examples of fruitful parish ministry told me he never asked anyone to do a task he was not prepared to do himself, whether this was cleaning out the church kitchen or breaking up concrete outside.

After invoking such a paradigm, I realize that my reader will ask: 'but how are we to attract the parish clergy we need?' and my answer will come in the next chapter under ordination training and Christian formation. Yet already it is evident that it will be hard to attract clergy with a pastoral heart to be oversight ministers of giant ministerial areas or hubs. It will also be hard to attract clergy to dioceses where there have been redundancies. Moreover, jobs should be manageable and not lead to clerical 'burnout'. Allowing the incumbent freedom and agency is much more likely to render the work satisfying and substantive.

The beginning of a mission strategy, however, for the Church, if it is to have a future, is intensity of attention to its core people and core activities, and for that purpose we need a simpler, less burdensome and clearer common life in which the local and the parochial has an honoured place.

7

The Crisis in Education and Communal Memory

My attention was drawn recently to a social media discussion about Tate and Lyle Golden Syrup, which has used the same famously iconic green tin design since the 1880s. Some young people had discovered with horror that the lion shown on the tin was actually dead. 'Out of the strong came forth sweetness', written on the tin is of course Samson's riddle in Judges 14, referring to bees making honey in the carcase of a lion he had killed with his bare hands when it attacked him.

I write, 'of course' and yet it is quite possible that many devout Anglicans, lay or ordained, may not have come across the story, given the very selective way the Bible is now used in worship. The image was used in medieval biblical exegesis typologically to refer to the resurrection and was part of the children's Ladybird version of Samson's story in my own youth, but it is now lost to cultural memory inside the Church as well as without.

This chapter is concerned with the collapse of biblical and theological literacy of which the Tate and Lyle tin is one example, across English culture from the clergy to the general public. It will suggest that, like the decline in church attendance, it was not as inevitable as is often assumed, and go on to advocate a renewal of Christian formation across the Church and in church schools, which can strengthen our witness and our parishes. I hope that sweetness may once again ensue from what may sometimes seem a decaying ecclesial carcase.

Church of England Schools

On its official website, the Church of England proudly announces that it educates currently over a million children in its schools. A quarter of all primary schools are Anglican, besides 228 secondary schools, and the website claims that 15 million people living today were educated in these schools and academies.[1] So how is it that 61% of children do not recognize the parable of the Good Samaritan, 40% have never heard or read of the crucifixion, while 46% of their parents did not realize that Noah's ark is part of a Bible story?[2]

These are a few of the shocking findings of a Bible Society report in 2014, which aimed to encourage parents to pass these stories on to their children. Even more shocking to me is that these stories are obviously not central to Church of England education. In my secular primary school in the 1960s we learnt a great deal about the Bible and actually read it. Our annual nativity play involved children narrating the story using the Authorized Version. Later, at my secondary school, we made model Bible libraries of individual books and studied St Paul's missionary journeys. I would not wish the somewhat wearisome detail with which we followed the indefatigable apostolic traveller's movements on today's pupils, but they are being deprived of the stories that formed their patrimony, which were once a natural part of the curriculum. Alasdair MacIntyre has written: 'Deprive children of stories and you leave them unscripted, anxious stutterers in their actions as in their words. Hence there is no way to give us an understanding of any society, including our own, except through the stock of stories which constitute its initial dramatic resources.'[3]

The irony is that these stories are not in and of themselves evangelistic tools and should therefore find a place in any school. The Bible Society has crafted the excellent 'Open the Book' assemblies, which offer over a hundred assemblies on different Bible stories, and which deliberately accord with Key Stage 2 and 3 learning outcomes, and are not imposed as evangelism, although discovering the richness of the Judeo-Christian tradition is itself an aid to human flourishing.

Over the years the Church of England has squandered its richness of access to children in not, at the very least, educating the children in its schools in the Scriptures. Faith schools do not have to follow the locally agreed RE syllabus, but even those syllabuses I have looked at offer ample space and opportunity for such teaching. Moreover, a faith school should surely also give its pupils some understanding of how the Bible works, its genres and organization, and it should offer practice in reading stories in the Bible itself, so that the narratives are anchored in context. Pupils should be taught some basic hermeneutics, so they can understand that the initial Genesis narratives are myths – stories to live inside and use as a lens to understand the world – and how other genres such as prophecy, history and gospels work.

So *why* has this detailed learning about the Bible not been central to the curriculum in our church schools? There are several reasons. First is the fact that many of those teaching the children do not know these stories themselves. Our problem is that communal memory is lost among adults and teachers feel unconfident about teaching such material. Secondly, teachers at primary level may not have specialized in RE, while the training of secondary RE specialists will have been Religious Studies in its methodology, with a presentation of religion by practices, worship and buildings alongside some minimal presentation of beliefs, which is unlikely to include a major study of the Bible. It is still possible to study the Bible for RE at A level but is very rarely attempted. Thirdly, although the Church of England offers a rich theological account of what education is for in its vision statement, hitherto it has offered no curriculum content about how these aims might be achieved. Too often the schools just follow the locally agreed RE syllabus rather than crafting their own, because it is a task for which they feel totally unqualified.

A fourth reason links to my analysis of the way confidence has been lost since the 1950s through a denigration of tradition and an anxiety about the nature of the faith and its promulgation. The Church educates children from a range of backgrounds and faiths and is often the only local school available. In such a context there has been a shying away from overt Christian content to the curriculum, lest Muslim children, for example, feel excluded or under pressure. Yet usually people of other faiths value enormously the fact that their children are in a religious school, and in the case of Jews and Muslims, many of the Old Testament/Hebrew Bible stories are shared. Hindus traditionally are extremely open to other religious stories and the Sikh scriptures themselves highly hospitable to figures and elements from other religious traditions.

Such concern, therefore seems misplaced, particularly when we are discussing the teaching of stories rather than doctrines. The latter should also form part of a Church of England RE curriculum, but in dedicated lessons, so that pupils may be properly formed by Christian teaching. A question-and-answer children's catechism, which could be learnt and used at home, would be a key pedagogical tool. We have lost this mode of formation, which once allowed the parish priest to teach and even employ it to teach children to read, while even the most hesitant parents could have a tool they could use with confidence.

There is good news to report because the Church herself has recognized that religious literacy in her schools and beyond is poor and has sponsored a recent programme, 'Understanding Christianity', which is focused around eight key Christian concepts and revisits these at different levels from age four to fourteen. There is a systematic attempt to present the 'big story' of the whole Bible and one of the most successful elements of the project is an artwork, *The Big Frieze* by Emma Yarlett, which embodies all the concepts and which children often pore over with fascination, pulling out new ideas as they develop in their learning.[4] The incarnation concept, for example, involves hearing about the Baptism of Christ and later the 'I am' sayings of John's Gospel and is very welcome for what it does. Yet being focused on key ideas, the programme does not seem to involve systematic Bible study or reading, or a great many Bible stories as narratives. It is written by a mixture of Anglican, non-Anglican and non-Christian teachers and it aims to be broad enough to be used in any kind of school. This is its strength, if secular schools could be persuaded to embrace it, but it does entail a less existential engagement with the themes than one might offer in a church school. It is a great step forward and let us hope that it will improve understanding of Christianity in the rising generation, but something like it should have been produced forty years ago.

Another way in which church schools fail to be Anglican is the dearth of Christian symbols in their buildings. My own local comprehensive is an ancient Christian foundation, but its new building marks this only by a sort of cross-shape evident only if you look closely at the notice marking the site. The Christian imaginary hardly makes an appearance. Instead of this lack-lustre absence, schools could offer a Christian plenitude. They could use liturgical colours to back work displays and shape the year with feast and fast recognition. Mothering Sunday with Mother Church included, Hallowe'en with All Saints emphasized, Candlemas, Pancake Day and Ashing on Ash Wednesday are all customs and festivals that can easily fit a primary or secondary calendar and be integrated with the cycles of the natural year, including Rogation and Lammas as well as Autumn Harvest Festival, which all schools tend to celebrate. Such festivities fit naturally into an ecologically aware curriculum, which is now universal, and help to promote what Pope Francis calls an 'integral ecology', not neglecting the human, nor presenting ecology as if it were a matter of cold, doom-laden disenchantment.

The national RE Council lays out its own understanding of the elements of curriculum that should be part of primary education, and these include using the arts to explore religious belief. So, a third way in which church schools at all levels could encourage religious literacy is through reading religious poetry, looking at the traditions of Christian art and music. Again, so much has been forgotten. In the 1960s, the BBC radio programmes 'Singing Together' and 'Rhythm and Melody' gave even schools without music specialists a grounding in music of many traditions, as well as English folk songs and carols. Think how useful such a resource would be today and how one could extend the global reach of such music so that Chinese, Nigerian and many other cultures could be represented. Primary-school children love to sing if they get the chance, but music is being drained from our culture as a performative, communal activity. A church school could also have access to a religious version of 'Singing Together', produced by our cathedral musicians, so that children learn every style of Christian music without any need of a resident specialist. All this study would help to cultivate a Christian imagination and bridge the cultural gap between church and society. It would really support the renewed work with choirs as part of missional outreach.

At the senior level, a church school should have a core series of art, music and literature that embodies Christian culture, and which is fed into the curriculum. Again, it used to be normal to sing *The Messiah* at school and I recall being an animal in Britten's *Noye's Fludde* aged eleven. We read C. S. Lewis children's fiction together at primary school and his adult *That Hideous Strength* as a critique of scientism at secondary school. This was in the 1960s and 70s – despite the cultural shift of those years, much continuity with an early period remained, and even the creative innovations of this period sometimes built on that, just as the brilliance of British Rock music of that time owed much to a sustained technical knowledge of how music works, derived in part from classical and folk idioms.

Much of the poetry we read, ancient and modern, had religious themes. One problem in education today is the flight from older literature, so that Christian writers such as Chaucer, the metaphysical poets, Milton, Wordsworth or Hopkins are little studied in comparison to recent writers. This is itself problematic, in that a culture without ancient roots lacks the ability to critique itself, to assess the pros and cons of past and present, and is highly fragile. All revolutions, including literary modernism, have reached back into the past for renewal – of which the Christian revolution is itself one example. While it is good to widen the range of cultural productions, this should not be at the expense of the great poetry and art of our past, which still can speak to us today.

Literary presentism also has the effect of exiling Christian culture from the curriculum, as so much of this rich material is religious. What alarms me as a university teacher is how wide the gulf has become between state and privately educated students. The latter have been inducted into a much denser and richer cultural curriculum, which is denied to ordinary children, and which gives the independently educated a great advantage at the university level in all humanities subjects, including Theology. It is no wonder that Christian parents, both Catholic and Protestant, are beginning to choose home-schooling (which has ambiguous implications for later socialization and engagement) in ever greater numbers.

Church schools, having made so little opportunity of their reach into British culture, are now potentially under threat in the new Academies legislation. The central Church seems to accept assurances from the government that the religious character of a church school in a non-religious academy grouping will be preserved, but some diocesan educationalists are worried. In December 2022 the Conservative Government withdrew its Schools Bill to make every school an academy but intends to return with new legislation, although it claims the religious foundation will be preserved. It is imperative, in my view, that the Church of England expedite a properly Anglican curriculum for RE and humanities, following the national RE Council but including Bible study, Christian doctrine and ethics, and the Christian imagination, for every level. They cannot enforce it on dioceses and schools, but what teacher would not make use of ready-made, high quality material with detailed lesson plans, were it made available?

It is all the more important to get this up and running before schools are hit with the demands of the 'world-view' approach to RE, where world religions will have to share RE with humanism and Marxism. There were only 10,000 self-identified Humanists in the 2021 census, far fewer than Jains (25,000), and fewer than in the previous census, but so aggressive is their self-promotion that they have already got themselves on the national Council's proposed curriculum and they are very much behind the move to World Views – even though humanism is not a positive world-view but merely negative atheism posing as such. Part of the logic of this new development is that RE is still too Christian in the terms in which it considers other faith traditions, and it aims to decentre RE from a 'Western' focus, as if Christianity were not equally, or in origins more, an Oriental creed, as Arthur Conan Doyle, along with many others in the late nineteenth century, came to realize.

Christianity is now growing in the far East and the global South, rendering all this warped perspective also increasingly ironic, but it is a threat that church schools need to be ready to address. A *genuinely* global perspective (not that of a decadent, disillusioned post-Christian West) and proper, rich accounts of other faiths in their complexity should be a feature of church school RE rather than a bland 'world-views' approach. The RE Council also give as one reason for its adoption of the latter the fact that an Islamic child may not recognize the Islam taught in the RE lesson, and yet to broaden the categories of description of what a world-view is will render the presentation of a particular religion even blander and vaguer, not to mention the fact that no Muslim would allow to atheist humanism any positive value whatsoever. A church school approach in which Christianity is taught in all its richness and specificity will make comparison with other religions more precise and interesting. It has been suggested that the 'Understanding Christianity' project be replicated for other religious traditions, which is a much more promising way forward.

One key element in the church school curriculum should be visits to the parish church and, if possible, the cathedral. Many clergy do welcome schools for services and spend time in their local school and there is nothing more effectively missional. But daytime school visits by a class with lay people showing them the different parts of the building and explaining the baptisms, marriages etc. that go on there has great value and should be frequent, with different aims for the various ages, and interdisciplinary in nature, so one year a nature or ecology theme, another architectural, and a further year historical and so forth could be adopted.

With the move to megaparishes or hubs, there is a tendency to employ a single lay chaplain across all schools in the group. While this might sound promising, it is likely to confine any outreach to the schools themselves and to sever the links with the locality, thus cutting the parish off from its school. There are examples where the children are linked only to a central resource church, which again divorces them from their local worshipping community. Parishes are being set up to fail here, when they could become a key resource for their local school. Parish clergy are thereby losing that precious access to their local schools which is one of the most important aspects of their ministry.

Church of England Ordination Training

We also have a crisis in ordination training, which has similarly lost a richness of content. I have already in the last chapter observed how little specific liturgical teaching and practice is carried out in training for Readers and lay ministers, but this is equally true of ordination courses. Parishes frequently tell me of how incoming clerics do not know how to use the Book of Common Prayer, even though it is included in their ordination oath. Yet the Prayer Book Society would work closely with theological colleges to support them in the acquiring of such expertise.

Ordinands are also increasingly ignorant of the theology of the sacraments. I recently celebrated a Common Worship teaching eucharist for a group of schoolchildren, many of whom had never been in a church, so you can imagine how simple my presentation had to be. Yet several young curates in attendance told me afterwards that what I had said was wholly new to them. They had never been given any sacramental theology of the most basic kind, and their tradition within Anglicanism had included little sacramental worship. And over the years ordination training has spent valuable time on faddish material, such as the Myers-Briggs tests, which have proved notoriously unreliable in experiments, have no grounding in clinical psychology, were devised by two amateurs, and reduce the human being to four letters.

Recently, I attended teaching sessions about the Daily Office and the expert leading them confirmed what I had suspected, which is that this too does not form part of many ordination courses, so that trainee clergy are not being formed in the range of the Scriptures that the daily lectionary offers, nor the discipline that it provides. Residential courses traditionally made this compulsory, so that by the time the student left it would be part of his or her character. My own ecumenical part-time course did include it as part of its weekends, but necessarily interwoven with patterns from other traditions and a great deal of so-called experimental worship – which too often involved stones or balloons – so that it did not become part of a rhythm. There is a significant number of ordinands who have come straight from free churches now being accepted for training, and who accordingly do not have parish formation, so that what is given in ordination preparation is even more vital. What I fear is that clergy are just not being trained for parish ministry and not being prepared for the pastoral role or the effective use of the occasional offices.

Liturgy is just one element of training that is simply not being attempted in many places, along with little about the history of liturgy and how our common worship evolved and what it means. The Common Awards syllabus, shared by all training schemes, does include modules on liturgy and sacramental theology, but either these are not being offered, or else they are taking a non-historical form. I note, for example, that the 'Christian Worship: Learning through Traditions' at St Mellitus and an equivalent module at Sarum are assessed by questionnaires and a reflection, which does not suggest an historical focus but just observation of different worship styles.

If residential training is being rationed ever more sparingly, those who follow part-time non-residential training would benefit from a short spell at a monastery or convent where they could learn liturgical patterns by an intensive immersion. It is not just that an incumbent undertakes to say the offices publicly and that they are enjoined on all clergy, but that they offer enormous benefit in shaping a job that can be inchoate and in providing calm and focus to a life that can be stressful and busy. The office connects the cleric with the rest of the church praying.

Liturgy is a cognitive as well as a spiritual exercise. In an article examining the neuroscience of liturgy, Hwarang Moon identifies a mode of practical learning that is unconscious but wholly formative, as well as the development of sensitization through habitual practices and four different modes of memory work that are at play.[5] Liturgical participation 'replicates the deep structure of biblical language' and helps us create meaning.[6] It was, he points out, the main mode of teaching in the early church. So, we are missing a central pedagogical tool if we underplay the importance of liturgical practice and its study in any educational programme that aims at forming Christians – not to mention downplaying liturgical forms in developing new worshipping communities. It is particularly important if the formation is of people less used to abstract, academic work. Shaped by liturgy, the student is already learning through the body, and this enables a natural step towards reflection and analysis.

At the same time, the amount of theological content has been greatly reduced in ordination training, as I indicated in Chapter Two. Far fewer ordinands are studying theology at university level as part of their training, and theology as such plays a reduced role throughout, mainly taking the form of reflection upon experience. While it is, indeed, important to internalize one's learning and think theologically in daily life, some content has to be given upon which to reflect and this is not always the case. I recall one irate and talented laywoman, whom I mentored in a diocesan 'Growing Faith' course, giving up in despair because she said they endlessly made her concentrate on her own life: 'I just want to learn about God,' she fumed.

Martyn Percy, who was formerly head of Ripon College Cuddesdon, an Anglican theological college, reports the following experience:

Some years ago, I was present at a meeting when the then most senior executive-manager in the Church of England told a gathering of our most senior theological educators that 'our days for doing theologies of education or for theological formation in training, or for church leadership, were over'. What he meant to suggest was this: that in the entire reconstruction of seminary or theological education, now imminent, there would be no theological thinking to reflect on the content or process of the new world being ushered in, or to construct the foundation upon which this new world would rest. All the decisions to be made were pragmatic, organizational and financial.[7]

There is a long history behind the move away from priestly and lay formation as induction into a tradition of thought and practice towards a more instrumental understanding. The *language* of formation, borrowed originally from Roman Catholicism, has been increasingly embraced, and this is wholly positive insofar as it implies that education is the shaping and transformation of the whole person. Words like *paideia* are used in the rationale for the Common Awards (courses validated by Durham, which all colleges offer), which refer back to ancient Greek ideas of education as training of the body and soul. Such training in the Platonic academy or Aristotelian school was, however, teleological, with defined aims and a body of knowledge to be acquired and a critical method of debate and self-questioning.

Under the guise of 'formation' too much theology has become in reality theological reflection, but often without the depth of engagement with doctrine, philosophy, liturgy or church history required to do such work. Yet a secular age all the more demands clergy who can account for their faith intellectually and empower their congregations to do so in their wake. We are not equipping clergy to do this or valuing such study. As I mentioned in the Introduction, John McGinley voiced a view to be found implicitly in many other recent Church reports, that clergy were 'limiting factors' on evangelism, precisely because their training, if residential, was long and cost money, as if educational formation were irrelevant to growth in the faith and its promulgation.

Far from diluting the content of the ordination training curriculum, we should be deepening it, because the apologetic task is necessary all the way through the life of the Church – as much at a funeral visit as at a synod. When religion as such is strange to a culture, as is increasingly the case, we have to start further back in our evangelizing endeavours. Before we can begin to present Christ, we need to argue for the metaphysical or the psychic and spiritual as such – that there is a depth to reality and to people beyond the purely material. Like Plato's philosopher in the myth of the cave, we need to reveal to people their chains and their taking of images for realities and lead them out into the light. We require philosophical theology in such a situation and the new apologetics programme that is beginning under Bishop Graham Tomlin, the Centre for Cultural Witness, is welcome. It needs to roll out a programme for every level: from primary school and upwards.

Currently, university departments of theology find their expertise rarely used. Two colleagues at different institutions from my own were asked at the last minute as a kind of rubber stamp to add a theological gloss to an Anglican report or policy of huge importance. In one case, hardly anyone on the committee even bothered to attend the theological presentation offered, and the report showed no evidence of having considered any underlying theology. On the other occasion, the academic just refused to endorse an already written report that lacked any theological basis.

My own Theology department used to offer regular study days for clergy and Readers, often based around the lectionary or other topics we thought they might find useful. We gave up because no one was interested. All this at a time when British theology has been singularly alive and well and in the case of the Radical Orthodoxy movement has been taking on the postmodernist turn in the humanities and social science and contesting secular disciplines on their own terms. Academic theology has made a number of recent converts, for there are those, like Dorothy Sayers, for whom ideas are the way to God. As her example shows, their subsequent influence on others who are intellectually inclined and very many who are not, is often then considerable. Ideas tend to trickle down from the top much more equitably than does money according to neo-liberal fantasy.

I look after the modern theological library at the cathedral where I assist, which is often given theological libraries owned by deceased or retiring clergy. We no longer accept them, because the generations who might have left collections of intellectual weight and value have given way to lightweight and often sentimental spirituality with no solid biblical commentaries or works of doctrine, modern or traditional. By contrast, the mature students who apply to study Nottingham University's rigorous distance masters' programme in systematic and philosophical theology are a joy to teach: eager to learn, intelligent and excited by the discipline. I am glad to say that some of them are even clergy, as are some of the equally highly motivated students of the Archbishop's doctoral programme, the AET. These, however, are the exception in a Church that increasingly views academic theology as elitist. It is, to the contrary, rather those who would deny ordinary Christians theological knowledge who are the elitists, helping to confirm the increasing constitution of class subordination by educational subordination in twenty-first century society.

Paradoxically, Pentecostal ministers, often working in secular jobs to fund their ministry, are often eager for academic theology and expose themselves to the riches of the Catholic and Eastern traditions with surprising open-mindedness. One reason for Anglican clerical neglect of theology may be the increasing busyness of clergy lives, running themselves ragged serving multiple parishes, but that does not excuse the lack of theological depth in training to begin with, nor the neglect by the hierarchy and church institutions.

Theology is an essential tool for ministry which the clergy are increasingly denied by the ecclesial hierarchy (with honourable exceptions). All the emphasis in Church reports is on 'missionary disciples', but the mission has to begin intellectually, for that is where the challenge lies. The new atheists have done their crude work of scientific positivism all too well and the younger generations have imbibed it. They have also grown up on a view of religion as (uniquely) causing violence, so that a deep knowledge of religious history is equally necessary for all of us, but especially clergy. To be truly humble, as *Vision and*

Strategy calls us to be, means admitting the wrong things the Church has done but also contextualizing them and giving a rich and nuanced account of our history, including the more fundamental things of which we should be ancestrally proud and for which we should be grateful to God.

We need highly trained and effective theologians among our clergy who understand that a chief ministerial task is to teach. One young parish priest told me recently that if we reduce ordination training further in terms of content, we will lack clergy capable of acting as training incumbents for the newly ordained. He sees a complete lack of understanding of what it is to work in a parish among those emerging from the newer schemes and lack of the theological expertise to help curates with their mentoring and post-ordination exercises. Diocesan internal training schemes, which provide training for some lay ministers and Readers, rely on such clergy for teaching, and their numbers are declining in a frightening way. I am still meeting young priests of real intellectual calibre and they are a blessing to the Church, and indeed it may be that *more* such people, reacting critically against the times they live in, are now potentially available, but their numbers will decline if the residential courses are removed, which is looking ever more likely, when so many of them face financial pressures and dioceses do not send them students.

From 2017 onwards, money for ordination training was funnelled through dioceses and very often they did not use it to fund residential training, which is one main reason why these colleges are struggling. Stephen Croft's report, which led to this change, claimed that this would not be the case, but in the first year there was a fall of 8%, and another 6% in the following, in residential study figures.[8] Bishops are favouring local courses with the justification that they are context-specific, but we are educating clergy to work throughout the Church of England, in diverse contexts, all of which will need background in biblical study, doctrine, philosophy, history and liturgical understanding as well as pastoral and evangelistic skills. While in 2023 modest new support for training colleges was proposed, it involved signing a Service Level Agreement to promote *Vision and Strategy*, which has not only never been openly debated and voted on, but which has within it the seeds of demise for ordained ministry as such.

In the last chapter I spoke of the gospel-teaching and service aspects of ministry, but these biblical roles are muted in the kind of training provided by the courses in the ascendent and in the pastoral reorganizations. Other professions are continually raising the amount of training given and expected, while the Church is evacuating its training of real content, sometimes in the mistaken belief that this will make it accessible. A foundation year is the way universities deal with students as yet unprepared for the standard university course, with transformative results in the case of my own institution, where those who have been though the foundation course do proportionally better in terms of the degree results finally gained than their peers in the degree programme. Their background and personal circumstances are often highly challenging. There is a foundation level to the Common Awards, but it shows little sign of being an equivalent to a university foundation course, which is intensive and directive.

Just as with our schools, we urgently need a common curriculum for ordination training. The argument against it is that there is no one form of ministry, but surely specialist modes should be offered post-ordination. Over a long career, traditionally a priest or other minister might work in very different contexts. With fewer clergy, we need people who can be flexible. Ian Paul, an evangelical, who formerly taught at St John's College, Nottingham lays out a possible core curriculum:

> In biblical studies, we need to engage with the Old Testament law, wisdom and prophetic writings, and understand the interpretative and theological issues in each. In New Testament, we need to engage in general and in depth with the gospels, Paul and the other epistles including Revelation.
>
> In doctrine and history, we need to understand key doctrines of Christology and atonement, and understand developments in the patristic and mediaeval periods, the Reformation, and the modern era. We need to understand liturgy, and have

enough philosophical background to make sense of the modern world.

In practical theology, we need to understand evangelism and mission, how to lead worship, how to preach (including why we are doing it!), issues around discipleship, learning and education, and the importance and practice of pastoral care.[9]

While I might want to add extra topics such as liturgy and philosophical theology, or indeed philosophy as such (with which all the great theologians of the past were fully familiar) this is surely a curriculum that all wings of churchmanship could embrace?

We need to find a way to enable everyone studying for the ordained ministry to first of all have a rich theological training, secondly, gain some proper parish experience and then thirdly, to have a period of sustained residence, in religious community or theological college, where habits of liturgical inculturation may be imbibed.

Formation of the Laity

Despite the denigration of theology in the Church of England at the upper levels and among ordinands themselves, if the anecdotal evidence several theological college lecturers have provided me with is to be believed, there is often a great hunger for theology among ordinary Christians, which is not to be met by holy books, useful in other ways though they are, when they are not just sentimental and misleading.

Just recently I have preached on some tough topics: the problem of evil; why we should lament; God as a violent character with passions in the Old Testament; is there a hell and is it eternal? I'm sure my attempts were imperfect in many ways, but they were greatly appreciated, simply because I spoke directly about tricky subjects and that is regarded as unusual.

Anglicans love to be nice, it is true (often far too nice), but they also like to think, and will often have been worrying away at some knotty theological issue on their own for ages. I once organized a weekend summer school programme on texts from the early church, which the lecturer, John Suddards, a learned parish priest who had devised the curriculum, and a co-dedicatee of this book, intended to make into a catechetical programme, so that the group taught would then become the teachers for others.

Those attending relished discussion about the *Didache* and its implications for parish life today, as well as what Athanasius's *On the Incarnation* had to say about how Christ saves us. None of them had a degree in theology and only a few had any higher education, but they were eager for substantive teaching. Of course, patristic texts are both prayerful and without too much technical language (compared with later scholasticism), which helped their understanding. This makes it all the more curious that Patristics (traditionally an Anglican bedrock) features so little in ordination training.

If we truly want a church of missionary disciples then we need to honour them and take them seriously, offering proper teaching in whatever form is appropriate, so that people can speak with confidence of the faith they hold. That is why we need highly educated clergy, who can present this to their congregations. Indeed, if we are to be missional, than our apologetics needs to be of high quality, whether it comes in the form of theological debate or my own preference for imaginative apologetics through the arts.[10] As with the children's formation, I think that a revised catechism, simple and direct, with question and answers, would be a good start for lay education and should include in it some specifically Anglican material, so that people know what it means to belong to our part of the Christian Church. It can be a resource in evangelistic outreach, giving ordinary Christians support and a quick point of reference.

In this regard one might ask why there is no Anglican equivalent of the Open University online, where anyone can study at a high level in their own time. Theologians would be delighted to support it and provide materials. The Christian faith is fortunate to have gifted artists, scientists and musicians, all of whom have much to offer and often see much more clearly the role of culture as outreach. They too could be part of this offering. Peter Howson in my Introduction is one such example of an artist, while the Anglican scientist Rupert Sheldrake is behind the formation of the British Pilgrimage Trust, the Choral Even-song Trust, and the revival of spiritual practices. New Christian converts, such as poet and novelist Paul Kingsnorth, have much to teach us, while the eminent Catholic composer Sir James MacMillan has also been generously involved in Anglican parish music-making. Not only are such witnesses compelling intellectually, but they have refreshingly particular ways of making our faith seem new and surprising.

If the Church is to have any future, she will have to intensify her communal life and render every activity more intentional, as if having a declamatory function. We need to make our own faith new and stress its refreshing difference. Education in the faith is one way in which people can understand rather than just passively accept their institution, its history and customs, its beliefs and practices, thereby encouraging more active participation.

One educational resource that we make little of is the body of retired clergy. The Church is happy to use them to take services: retired clergy, I was informed by one such, are all that keeps the Church in Wales going, now they have carved up the land into huge mission areas. Yet how often are they used as tutors for ordinands, or consulted for their wisdom and experience? Retired clergy have the right to stand as representatives of their peers, in synod elections at every level, but how often do dioceses make that a reality by setting up such electoral colleges to elect retired clergy?

We sorely need the confidence that comes from being rooted in a tradition and having something upon which to depend and our failure to make full use of our retired clergy is evidence of this. What we are denying everyone whom we teach from small children to ordinands is a sustaining tradition. Simone Weil wrote of this need in the dark days of World War II:

> The opposition of future to past is absurd. The future brings us nothing, gives us nothing; it is we who in order to build it

have to give it everything, our very life. But to be able to give, one has to possess; and we possess no other life, no other living sap, than the treasures stored up from the past and digested, assimilated and created afresh by us. Of all the human soul's needs, none is more vital than this one of the past.[11]

Weil had in mind occupied France, cut off from its political and religious traditions, but our society is increasingly as vertiginous and deracinated. From schoolchildren to clerics we all need the security of knowing that 'we enter upon a stage which we did not design and we find ourselves part of an action that was not of our making'.[12]

To be educated in our faith as deeply as we are able gives us what MacIntyre refers to as 'the narrative unity of a life'. In Christianity this is not the self-shaping of an individual, but an awareness of being storied, of inhabiting an historical narrative with an eschatological goal. 'What is better or worse for X depends upon the character of that intelligible narrative that provides X's life with its unity', MacIntyre writes and 'it is the lack of any such unifying conception of a human life which underlies modern denials of the factual character of moral judgments'.[13]

We have a moral crisis in that our society still, as Tom Holland has pointed out, relies on Christian ethics for its understanding of value, without inhabiting the Christian narrative or anthropology.[14] It has literally lost the plot. It is not too late, in my view, to seek to restore some of the richness of Christian heritage and moral claims to education at every level, in school, parish and seminary, for we have the academics, the artists, poets and musicians to aid us, but the task is pressing and urgent. However, as a recent article by Imogen Sinclair in the *New Statesman* demonstrates, Generation Z shows signs of a desire to return to tradition, so that we might find a more receptive audience among young people than we imagine.[15]

8

Kill the Parish?

Is Decline Inevitable?

In the previous two chapters we saw how the parish is being squeezed by a collapsing of the value of different layers of authority and how its people are being short-changed by a failure to teach the full riches of the Christian tradition. The outlook for the Church is grave.

My present chapter title is the name of a Swedish heavy metal group founded in 1997 in imitation of the Norwegian Black Metal bands, who were not only Satanist in belief but, in some cases, carried out the destruction of actual parish churches on the grounds that they usurped the ground of former pagan shrines (although of the twenty or so arson attacks performed there were few that actually met this criterion).[1]

There are a number of voices within the Church of England, who would similarly like to destroy the whole Church structure and start again. Here is Ian Paul, whom I quoted earlier as urging a strong curriculum for clerical training, but who is recently writing: 'The church in its present form will have to die. It is dying. It's slow and drawn out because we don't have the nerve, or the structures, to make clear and painful decisions.'[2]

To which the obvious and surely correct secular response would be: 'you are deceiving yourself if you think that the decline of the parish is not the decline of Christianity as such'. But a further corrective response, which this entire book proposes, is that while the parish is integral to Christianity, the decline of neither is inevitable. The scale of recent decline is to a degree self-inflicted and inflicted precisely because of the embrace of the dangerous illusion and false alibi that supposes that a more exciting faith can emerge from the parish's demise. In reality, the Christian exponents of a 'soft metal' outlook do the work of the hard metal neo-Aryans more effectively than Satanic arson attacks.

Covid has been an opportunity to expedite further the soft-Satanic demise of traditional church, as in this extract from an article by some senior clergy in the *Church Times*:

> Being prevented from 'going to church' might liberate us from our habitual routines to 'become church' all over again – or, perhaps, for the very first time. Such rejuvenation may help to release us, at last, from the prison of our church building which, for many, have become shrines to the past which not only soak up energy and resources, but also perpetuate concepts of division and hierarchy harmful to a mature understanding of who we are.[3]

As I argued in Chapter 6, hierarchy itself is inescapable and the important criterion is that a hierarchy be virtuous and dynamic. But this whole passage is redolent of fond fantasy, scornful of the material and the incarnational and so scornful of the heart of Christianity itself. In this book I have demonstrated how back in reality a range of factors have impacted badly on parochial ministry: command-and-control managerialism, incoherent ecclesiology that assumes it can combine a gathered and open church in one institution, mission policies that have direct and negative effects on parishes, direction of resources away from parishes to administration and SDF projects, churches denied incumbents in ever lengthening interregna, failure to invest in thorough ordination training that prepares ordinands for parish work, a downgrading of the ordained ministry itself. It is a wonder that parish ministry is as vibrant as it is given a loss of belief in its value, which I have traced back to the 1960s.

For up and down the country there are flourishing and lively parish churches, which give the lie to an entirely negative entire picture, but only because the richly successful Anglicanism of the first half the twentieth century has obstinately survived, in the face of much resistance.

When Johannes Arens came to St Andrew's Leicester in 2019, this erstwhile Anglo-Catholic beacon had lost much of its local population by redevelopment and its congregation was almost in single figures. Now, it is heaving with a worshipping community of two hundred of all ages derived from many ethnicities and cultures. Campbell Paget from an evangelical background has similar success with parochial ministry in a village context at Brenchley in Kent, as he did formerly in a deprived area of Chatham, with hundreds in his congregation and thriving youthwork. In London, I have attended a number of full and successful traditional churches across the city from Ealing to Catford. In my own area of rural Nottinghamshire, when St Bartholomew Kneesall was threatened with closure, the widow of its former churchwarden went round the village putting up notices and working to keep the church, which was already half a village hall, alive. Six months later, services in a village of 350 attract an average of between 40 and 90 people. The local café serves refreshments and an anthem is sung by a choir: the Kneesall Knightingales, started by a newly arrived piano teacher.

The reasons why some churches succeed and others struggle are many and varied. In his wise study of the missional value of pastoral work, Paul Avis points out that the biblical parable of the Sower assumes that there may, indeed, be stony ground, inimical to the gospel, but also that what may seem like failure may have sown seeds that will only break the soil many years later.[4] Apart from the Kneesall example, where at present they inhabit a kind of liminal state awaiting reorganization, the other parishes I mention all have a priest to themselves and that is the key (unlimiting!) factor in halting decline. Although in itself a resident vicar is not a recipe for a flourishing church, without it decline is likely, as *From Anecdote to Evidence* showed only too clearly. We have seen old-established free church denominations withdraw more and more from the countryside, until they become primarily suburban churches, in sad disparagement of many fine traditions of rural resistance. As Paul Avis writes, 'Proposals to merge parishes, combine PCCs and close church buildings are usually profoundly misguided. Centralized paternalism is a stock recipe for decline.'[5]

We still have a choice about whether there will be a parochial ministry in the future. Tiffer Robinson wrote about his own diocese of St Edmundsbury and Ipswich to describe the change that came about when a new bishop arrived six years ago:

> He announced soon after he arrived that the policy of cutting clergy posts to meet our shortfall in parish share was a plan for decline, and not for flourishing. Instead, for the past five years, our diocese has sought to counter a chronic annual deficit of around half a million through increasing giving and encouraging growth.[6]

This appears to have succeeded, because it was accompanied by support for parishes, not chastisement for those unable to pay their full share, a genuinely pastoral senior ministry team and real valuing of clergy and local ministry.

I have already alluded to a change in strategy in Chelmsford, under Bishop Giuli, although the ending of the Darlow Formula allowance in favour of SDF funding led to a cut from £3.1 million to 1 million that had been catastrophic for that diocese, leading to clerical redundancies under the then bishop, Stephen Cottrell. Part of the new financial arrangements were in the form of Lowest Income Community Funding, but these were given to each diocese to award, and only 40% eventually found its way to the poorest 10% of parishes overall throughout the English dioceses.

Another diocese that shows confidence in parish ministry is Blackburn, which is far from having the kind of financial reserves some ancient dioceses enjoy. In September 2021 its bishops stated: 'As a diocese we remain committed to parish life, to maintaining our current numbers of stipendiary clergy, to forming excellent priests and lay leaders and to investing in the front line.'[7] The then Bishop of Burnley, Philip North, continued to point out that parishes pay for the ministry they receive, so that cutting ten priests means losing ten stipends in contributions. It is a recipe for decline. While in this same report he drew attention to how poor leadership and wrangling can destroy parish life, he was emphatic about the need for confidence: 'And, when the messages you are giving out are: "Oh, we are in trouble, decline is inevitable, we have to embrace the future", the future becomes the thing of threat, morale goes down, and parishes stultify.'[8]

How to Save the Parish: National Conversations

In *For the Parish* Andrew Davison and I spent several chapters laying out the value of parishes, a model of parochial mission and an ethics of liturgical personhood, as well as a chapter on how to be missional in parish life. Among the contributions of the parish system, we enumerated the values of stability, echoing the eternal rock-like stability of God, the honouring of a place as having value, which is particularly important in areas of deprivation, besides the importance of the local and relational, inclusivity, the church as refuge, sacrality, a mediating structure.[9]

So, what specific initiatives will enable the parish system to continue? There are a variety of levels at which to address this question, from the national to the local. First, nationally we need some way of addressing the burden of repairs on historic churches and a public conversation about the way forward. In the thirteenth century there was a new move to grant English parishioners responsibility for the upkeep of the nave of their church, which had hitherto been the incumbent's task.[10] It might seem an oppressive move, given that the laity already paid tithes to support their priest, but it was a policy resisted by some bishops, lest they lose control of the building. This suggests there was some lay appetite for having a degree of responsibility for and control over their own church.

It is a miracle that our parish churches today as a whole are in such good repair, given the central role of local people in maintaining them. In 2021 the tiny parish of one hundred souls in Owston in Leicestershire raised £95,000 to repair the spire, tower and east window of their church, and in 2022 another £21,000 to repair a bulge in the east wall, all without any support from the diocese.[11] The parishioners do this heroic work with great devotion, and one would not want to remove agency wholly from them. They do, however, need greater support so that not all their energies are put into maintenance. Yet the dedicated religious building stream of National Lottery Funding has been removed quite recently, which is really unfair given that churches make up 45% of all Grade 1 listed buildings in the country. That 'place of worship' stream should be restored and extended.

There should also be national resources and information on which parishes could draw for grant application, which is professional work. Cathedrals often employ heritage experts to guide them through the process and such expertise ought in some way to be available to local churches. I am delighted that the Centre for Christianity and Culture at York is planning an online resource to guide parishes through the labyrinths of grant application. This is an area in which the diocesan DAC's advice could be supplemented by national resources, with specimen successful applications. Furthermore, this is yet another area where academics can be useful, including those outside the specialisms of archaeology and architecture. University academics all spend much of our lives drafting grant applications for funding and the technique is, as they say, a transferable skill. Universities are anxious to prove they offer knowledge-exchange and impact, so will be willing to help, as the benefit is mutual. It also has outreach benefit for the parish in making a relationship with a local institution, which may even tie the project into its curricula and arrange student visits.

A second aim of a national conversation would look at the possibility of a Church Commissioners' endowment, matched by the government, to be drawn on in cases of especial need or largeness of scale. The Commissioners have recently made a grant of £100 million to a fund to address the historical damage of slavery and one might see my proposed endowment as a way of acknowledging the tithed working classes' contribution to making and supporting these buildings in the past. Queen Anne's Bounty, the source of much Church Commissioners' money (not to mention the glebe taken into diocesan hands in 1976) was intended for poor parishes. A secular state like France is responsible for the upkeep of cathedrals nationally and 90% of parish churches through the commune. Other European countries have church taxes.[12] These latter are of long standing and are unlikely to fly in an increasingly secular Britain, although the contribution of non-churchgoers to the maintenance of their parish church is considerable and essential to their survival. This too can be considered a point of outreach. Indeed, I know of several recent examples of people without any Christian faith who have been drawn into the life and worship of their parish church through a threat to its upkeep or existence.

Although, as I write, there is a severe cost of living crisis and therefore the time seems unpropitious for any government outlay, when need is so great elsewhere, the importance of parish churches as part of the social and community service is all the more important. The National Churches Trust puts the value of all church social service at an annual £55 billion and without that parish network of support, much more government money would be expended.[13] The Trussell Trust foodbanks alone, in which many churches are involved, are a major preventer of hunger in a society in which even some of those in work struggle to feed their families. Self-interest should motivate government action if nothing else.

While maintaining their resources for the future, the Church Commissioners could also be asked to redirect much of the money they give out in SDF/SMMI funding towards parishes in the form of clergy and to real theological education that will give us the confident, well-trained clergy that we need. Along with that money for outreach projects could be provided, especially in outer estates, but more closely connected to the parish system.

How to Save the Parish: Diocesan Administration

As has already been argued, we need a simpler diocesan administrative structure, with centralizing of some functions, to lift the burden locally and gain economy of scale. The rise of dioceses as administrative entities has already been outlined, as well as their growth, with the worst examples having almost as many central diocesan employees as stipendiary parish clergy. Part of the reason for their size, however, apart from the managerialism outlined in Chapter Four, is first, the rage for communication and its policing, secondly, the need to show compliance with safeguarding, health and safety etc. and, thirdly, the reorganization agendum itself.

With regard to communication, I have already suggested that bishops should say less, so that their interventions have more weight, and this should be reflected throughout diocesan communications generally. The thinking behind the social media policy seems to be that any active organization has to update its social media constantly, but this is not the case. Working out the purpose and audience of social media and other communications would quickly demonstrate that fewer communications with more real content are preferable.

Safeguarding, given the woeful failures of the past, matters, but it is not clear that the way it is being done, with everyone from the PCC treasurer to the church opener trained every three years, prevents abuse, which is ultimately grounded in a failing culture and can be resistant to formal checks. In my own diocese, training is delivered by gifted individuals, but the material they are made to present has highly problematic elements, not least the way the Bible is sometimes used.

When one looks at past errors in dealing with examples of abuse, they are to do with those in authority, especially clergy and bishops. Yet in some dioceses lay volunteers are made to do three training events every three years and repeat training if they take on different roles. All this seems to have more to do with *protection of the institution from accusations* than with actually ensuring the safety of children or vulnerable adults. It so dominates that we now have a dedicated 'Safeguarding Sunday' and a kind of perversely sacralized pathologizing of relationships. In the older examples of abuse that I know about, lay people were quick to spot a problem and report it without any training whatsoever. In two cases (fortunately not recent) the bishop failed to act appropriately. It is clergy, especially those in deanery or diocesan roles, who really need to be educated in this respect. Indeed, the stringent requirements on parishes contrast with the lack of proper training and procedures at Lambeth Palace itself, which were revealed by an SCIE audit in 2022.

At present, each diocese is doing its own version of safeguarding training, but there is, at last, a commitment to a national recording system, the National Safeguarding Casework Management System (NSCM), and a roll-out of a national learning framework. Yet in this new order, PCC members have to 'have a due regard' for church policy, which means that they must immediately start training once they are appointed.[14] Instead of a yearly check-up on policy at a PCC meeting with a practical example to discuss as a body, each individual must do training, and this puts a great strain on parishes seeking to attract new volunteers.

The Church of England's implausible response in *Safeguarding: Learning and Development* is to say that people must stop seeing this training as an imposition and internalize safeguarding as part of their ecclesial DNA. The problem with this approach is that it depends on a virtue ethics approach to behaviour, where one learns a virtue by habit until what had formerly been difficult becomes delightful and easy through practice: like learning a musical instrument. A virtue, however, is a positive quality or disposition, whereas safeguarding is prevention of something negative: harm or abuse. It requires embedding in a broader, more theological account of positive flourishing for it to be easily internalized – indeed, what I would call a parochial anthropology of interconnectedness and mutual care. We need a more positive account of human flourishing to undergird the care of the vulnerable and avoid the oppression of the bully and the abuser.

So, the writers of the Anglican safeguarding document are quite right to stress the importance of internalizing learning, but that learning needs to be more holistic. If safeguarding could be integrated into other learning, it would be more effective and less intimidating, especially to ordinary lay people. It would need fewer paid safeguarding trainers and the central recording system should lessen the administrative burden on dioceses. The operation of the subsidiarist principle of operating at the most feasibly appropriate level often requires more geographical devolution in most integrated matters and yet *more* central coordination of certain sectoral issues common to a whole nation and largely indifferent to local variation.

My third point, that the pastoral reorganization and mission initiatives cause a bloated diocesan structure has already been demonstrated. It is costly and complicated to change parish structures and uses energies that could be more productively employed. Moreover, the diocesan and national church bureaucracies engender work that places heavy administrative burdens on parish clergy, demanding endless form-filling by incumbents, which a larger administration in any institution tends to generate. The diocese can help with a faculty, legal advice or a new appointment, but the traction in a top-heavy bureaucracy always tends towards making the front-line workers serve it rather than the other way round.

How to Save the Parish: Responding to Social Needs

If you sat down and thought about the great problems that face us today, they might include some of the following, garnered from people I encountered today out shopping in the market. They told me that our social care system is practically defunct and old people are being neglected. The gap between rich and poor has widened, and many, even in work, cannot afford even to eat properly or enjoy safe and healthy housing. There is an unparalleled crisis of mental health among our young people, and they are lonelier and often poorer than ever before. Ukraine's invasion returns war to our own continent, without mentioning the many other conflicts in the world. They lament the instability caused by climate change and species decline. There is also the problem about how best to respond to migration and what really motivates it in such unprecedented numbers. Generally, my respondents agreed that we have lost our sense of direction and our moral compass. We no longer have any basis on which authority can be exercised. I could go on.

Parish Potential: Poverty and Social Needs

Far from being some fusty irrelevant institution belonging to the past, to every one of these challenges the parish offers some sort of positive response. I have just met a concerned parishioner this morning who has been working tirelessly on behalf of the old and sick for years in consultation and research projects with the NHS, and who offers a significant personal ministry among the elderly here in Southwell. She is not alone. I spotted one nonagenarian from my kitchen window out and about every day during lockdown, despite the advice to stay inside as one of the vulnerable. She was busy doing errands for the house-bound. Parishes up and down the country respond to poverty with foodbanks, advice centres and deliveries. I think of Father Alex Frost, whom many may have heard of after he and the amazing Pastor Mick were featured on the BBC in 2020 for their work among the poor in Burnley. Some pews were later removed from Father Alex's church, St Matthews, to make way for tables, as they offer cooked meals to the hungry, after having started their own foodbank during lockdown. Food-banks are not the answer to economic hardship, as those who work in them are all too aware, but they are a lifeline.

The National Churches Trust report *The Future of the UK's Church Buildings* lists a range of social service projects in churches up and down the land, from drug and alcohol coun-selling to youth groups, while the ResPublica report, *Holistic Mission*, which was commissioned by the Church of England, found that 81% of respondents to its survey of practising Anglicans stated that they get involved in social action in their communities because of their faith; 79% of respondents had been involved in social action in the past 12 months.[15] In the report's foreword, Tom Jackson of Resurgo Social Ventures writes:

Local churches are distinctive in their geographic spread across the country, their commitment to social service and their ability to catalyse a local network of volunteers. Churches therefore provide a critical platform for deep social transformation and could generate even greater social impact with bolder vision, resourcing and leadership.[16]

Where national institutions such as the NHS struggle, partly from short staffing, but also from their unwieldy centralized structures, intermediate bodies such as the parish are much more responsive to local needs. The ResPublica report cites an article by Adam Dinham:

> While all the Christian churches, and many faiths which are newer to Britain, are active in communities, it is suggested that the Church of England in particular has been effective in communities by deploying its national scope locally through its wide-reaching networks of staff, buildings and resources in every part of the country, even where other actors and agencies have withdrawn.[17]

The key element here is locality and depth of knowledge of particular communities. Furthermore, as the Revd Jimmy Hutton from St Stephen's Bradford observes, when the government funding for a particular project dries up, the work ends, whereas 'a local parish is committed to its community always'.[18] His church offers food, internet access and job counselling as well as constant supplies of hot drinks and a listening ear year in year out.

Parish Potential: the Ecological Crisis

The crisis of climate change and more general environmental dereliction is both a challenge and an opportunity for the parish, precisely because of its geographical definition, embracing an area of land, air, energy and water as well as people and businesses. The cure of souls has often in Anglican history been extended to nature, whether in the case of the parson-naturalists of the past, or contemporary priests influenced by the new nature writing, such as Colin Heber-Percy in *Tales from a Country Parish* and Andrew Rumsey in *English Grounds*. Parish, as Andrew

Rumsey points out in his earlier book of that name, is a potent word, since it refers not just to a group of people, but to a kind of cosmos in miniature.[19] Naturalist Richard Mabey notes in his new introduction to it that Gilbert White's *Natural History and Antiquities of Selborne* is an account of the whole parish in both space and time, uniting nature and culture, as the rarely used full title, including antiquities, makes plain.[20]

'Parish' is a favoured word for the Common Ground charity not only because of its stress on the local as the site for transformative action but also because it carries a sense of value and of care. Indeed, the host of ecological projects under way in parishes up and down the land is extensive, and 250 parishes, for example, took part in A Rocha's Churchyard Countdown on Nature last year, including St Michael's Aldbourne, which invited the local church primary school to a day's workshop and involved 230 children. After counting species such as slow-worms and butterflies, the children hunted for hidden stones with words on them, which collectively spelt out Psalm 24.1: 'The earth is the Lord's and everything in it.'[21] Projects like this lead to community outreach and presentation of the gospel, here in the form of a theology of creation.

The response of the Church of England to the climate change crisis has been primarily one of dubiously limited and debatable target-setting, which has engendered some resentment in impoverished parishes and those with draughty churches who are not allowed to replace a boiler, even though its once weekly use is hardly a threat to global warming. Yet, as with safeguarding, the parochial vision is a way to turn this whole process into something positive, building on the desire to save our local ecology for its own sake and for the sake of the cherishing of the named, visited and particular, which is more likely to elicit local support. I have had a small part in an innovative international project, 'Learning by Doing', under the leadership of the inspirational head of the Mexican NGO, Energeia, Jose Garibaldi, made up of climate scientists and predictors as well as theologians and artists, who all realize that targets are not enough: we require new anthropology, a human way of being that will make us capable of living sustainably. The monastic and the parochial communities are studied by this group because of their potential to change desire and reorder the human telos to the common good through the imagination and an awareness of beauty and sacrality.

If we are as a country going to respond appropriately to the crisis we face, the way forward is primarily local and parochial, in contexts where people can see the effects of species-deprivation or climate change on their own habitats, whether urban or rural. It will involve a change in the way we understand the purpose of human life as interdependent and primarily local and subsidiarist in its exchanges and use of resources. That is going to be the key for real change, and it is no wonder that so many naturalists and ecologists are aware of this fact.

Parish Potential: Loneliness and Mental Health

The parish is self-evidently a place for community: Oliver O'Donovan more precisely describes it as a mode of gathering. It comes into its own at times of danger or crisis, with Tewkesbury Abbey sheltering local people from flooding, or St Clement Notting Dale offering support to those affected by the Grenfell Tower conflagration. The parish system enabled swift, practical response and effective representation for people who still struggle to get justice. St Clement had a long tradition of community involvement, leading to an associated charity, as well as strong relationships with the local mosque. More recently, parish churches all over the country have been offering warm spaces at a time of high energy costs. In the examples I have visited it has been companionship as well as economics that have drawn people to them, as well as quiet places to work.

The parish nurse initiative brings professional support to informal parochial support for the ill and lonely, and often energizes teams of volunteers to work with them in offering a holistic approach to health and wellbeing. Here is an example from St Michael's Church, Camden: 'This service seeks to support regular and occasional church attenders, as well as those who engage with groups that the Parish offer, such as the gardening group that supports those with mental health concerns and offers outreach to the homeless and others who congregate around the church premises.'[22]

It is sad that the United Kingdom is one of the regions in which young people are most separated from other generations, much more so than in other European countries. While it is important to focus outreach to children and teenagers, given the paucity of their numbers in our churches, if we are to really respond to their needs we need to offer opportunities for them to be part of wider society. This is where the parish is once more key in being able to offer roles for children and young people from serving as boat-boys or girls, as acolytes, singing in choirs, bell-ringing and being part of a mixed community. I am amused when I see 'choir church' touted as a new worshipping community or fresh expression, when it was the norm for most churches until the 1970s.

At St Wulfram's Grantham, a strongly working-class town, they are lucky to have a choir director who offers a weekly music lesson in each of the town's primary schools and from this base has recruited forty children for the church choir, who sing one service a week. There were twenty-five of them on the occasion when I heard them in action and they sing, of course, with adults. In the 2017 report from the Centre for Church and Community, choir club was an a factor in encouraging growth in two of the seven parishes studied: St John's, Catford and St George's in the East.[23] A recent glance at St George's website shows real imagination in making links with the local primary school, whereby not only do the children sing but the whole school gets involved in justice and social service projects encouraged by the church – so once again the children are being connected to the adult congregation and the wider community.[24]

From my experience as a university academic, young people are increasingly isolated from each other: even traditionally well-connected students. A recent set of seminars on the virtue of friendship in Aristotle, which used to be popular with students comparing their own friendships to his taxonomy of utility, pleasure and virtue, failed completely, because they now seem to struggle even to articulate an ethic for relationships. I note how many of them come singly to class, where formerly they came bunched in groups. Anxiety and depression are states articulated by the majority in tutorial meetings.

It is, however, noticeable how those who have a faith-adherence are not only less likely to present with anxiety but remain socially connected: this is as true of Catholic students as those in the Christian Union. A recent event at a highly traditional Prayer Book parish church in York revealed a significant community of students as part of its congregation. I pointed out in the last chapter how, in the megaparishes now being developed in Leicester and Truro, the model followed is often a dedicated chaplain to schools, with either an understanding that the school becomes the 'church' or a link with one youth-focused church, thus setting up the local churches to fail, as the young people are creamed off – along with an ultimate viable future. Yet a mixed community is much more likely to allow a young person to grow and develop. While it is helpful to have some critical mass of young people in a congregation, the presence of children and older people is much more stable. Consistent anecdotal evidence suggests that the youth megachurch is less likely to lead to sustained commitment. Above all, the peace of the local church and the rhythms of its worship are healing in themselves.

Parish Potential: Migrants

One of the accusations made against the parish is that it assumes longevity of dwelling. What about the transient and the migrant? Yet if you are a refugee, what you seek is some stability, as I found in the initial influx of those fleeing the war in Ukraine. They were drawn to the cathedral as a holy place with ancient stones and I prayed with several arrivals, who incidentally seemed to experience an immediate resonance between Anglicanism and their own Orthodoxy or Eastern-rite Catholicism. A migrant from Romania sought baptism at the cathedral and was gently redirected to her own local Anglican parish church.

There she was given a warm welcome and she is now an active member of their congregation. We invited her back to the cathedral to be Mary with her new baby in our nativity play.

An (unnamed) village church in the Leeds diocese reported to Save the Parish about their Christmas services and outreach and added: 'The church and village have contributed a substantial amount of food for our nearest food bank in the run-up to Christmas, and we have several Ukrainian refugee families staying with us. The church is the major focal point for the community at Christmas, and saving the parish is vital for all the residents and not just for those who worship regularly.'[25] In my own county similarly, it is churches who are particularly active in supporting asylum seekers, who are often not able to work until their claims are decided.

We all need roots, wherever we are, and our pilgrim nature as Christians does not imply that we should have no roots on this earth but that they should themselves be rooted in Christ, the Word who shapes creation every moment and who has given himself to the earth forever. I have already quoted Simone Weil's *The Need for Roots*, which was commissioned in 1943 as a blueprint for reconstruction of France after the war. Weil had especially in mind the industrial working-class. Too often they had been displaced by unemployment. and experienced a particular need to have a past and a tradition, from which one can send out shoots of connection: 'Rooting in and the multiplying of contacts are complementary to one another.'[26] Displaced workers and immigrants are as anxious to 'root in' as anyone else and in fact, more so.

Sadly, in the first wave of immigration from the Caribbean, uncomprehending and sometimes racist congregations froze out their fellow Anglicans who were trying to root in. Yet today our churches in many cities not only appreciate but are now reliant on their African and Caribbean-heritage faithful; it is waves of recent immigration that probably give London its rise in worshipping numbers. Similarly, in Manchester, for example, migrant Iranians form the backbone of some urban parish churches, so that we are now witnessing a healthy number of vocations to the priesthood from their number. We have had bishops, and even an archbishop, who came here as refugees. John Sentamu left Uganda after speaking out against Idi Amin, while the already cited Bishop of Chelmsford, Revd Giuli Francis-Dehqani, fled Iran with her family when she was just 14, in 1980. St Andrew's Leicester, again already mentioned, which rejoices in over twenty nationalities within its congregation, is blessed with a good proportion of nurses from Kerala in South India.

Holy Innocents, Fallowfield, in Manchester first met Iranian asylum seekers who had been housed near the back of the church and now have a flourishing Iranian community among their worshippers, who have since gained right to remain:

> We are not simply a multi-cultural congregation; we are also rooted in place. There is an Iranian language Church in south Manchester, and some Farsi members have tried it or were aware of it, but they chose to come to us instead. These are people working with their new identities as both Iranian and British with all its complexity. It is much more than just being multi-cultural, it is also rooted in the cultures of Anglicanism and living in Manchester. Teasing out how that blend works is an ongoing conversation.[27]

So up and down the country migrants are actually reviving our parishes, especially in the inner cities. We are returning to one of the earliest understandings of *paroikia* in the early church as the sojourning place, in which migrants among us remind us of the fact that we are all sojourners on this earth, with a heavenly destination.

War was mentioned by my random sample of lay Anglicans, and I cannot pretend that the parish can solve international problems. Yet it is a key place for articulation of the need for reconciliation and peace-making, which must begin with ourselves. From the time of the *Didache* at the end of the first century, with its discussion of the need for reconciliation before coming to share the Eucharist, to the divides between villagers today, the local church is committed to this work. Returning to the United Kingdom from working in the USA, I was immediately struck by the breadth of concern in ordinary parish church intercessions. Many episcopal churches, by contrast, do not mention anywhere beyond America's shores. But here even the most remote of parishes will not fail to remember Ukraine, while the energy crisis of the period at which I write is a constant concern. It is in their prayer that parishes show what really matters to them and the long lists of the sick and bereaved are very powerful. On a recent visit to the Yorkshire Dales, I found a church locked, yet it had a large open porch where people could pray, with intercession cards, a candle-stand and no fewer than three separate places for collections: foodbank, clothing for asylum seekers and the Ukraine.

During the pandemic, the Common Good Foundation released a plea to the parish. The coronavirus and lockdown revealed its value as never before:

> The places denuded of value and purpose are revealed again as a site of meaning, a place where people live and from which they work. The parish has returned as a site of living community, with its land and nature, its character and history, its wounds and its promise. It is the elemental theatre of living m community. Its institutions and buildings, including churches, are no longer abandoned monuments to inevitable decline but full of necessity and hope and the new chapter is played out within its bounds. People and place matter in this story. Their particularity is transcendent.[28]

The document predicts, in a biblical analogy, a famine after the plague and its words are prophetic. Like all institutions in this time of scarcity, the Church is vulnerable: 'It can be merged and bought out. Its redemption is found in its friends and neighbours "of this parish", who are also vulnerable and anxious. In relationship, it becomes stronger. In doing things together it brings meaning to locality, it rewrites its history.' But by every index of relevance to human need, the parish has value, as I have briefly sought to indicate. The Foundation's *The Plague and the Parish* locates a sustainable future for the parish in its relationships with every other aspect of its locality, which are similarly fragile.

My final area of concern among local people was a breakdown of any objective value discernible in society at large. As the late Pope Benedict XVI said in his speech in Westminster Hall: 'By appeal to what authority can moral dilemmas be resolved?'[29] We need a restoration of the idea of the Common Good, which can only be located in a divine basis to society, a metaphysically objective good that is not merely a human invention and so can hold us to account. Here again we can make common cause with people of other faiths and with those who adhere to the good implicitly, even if they cannot name it or are cautious about naming it, so that their genuine agnosticism has some kinship with that negative theology that is intrinsic to Christian faith. Although the recent census returns revealed fewer Christians and many of 'no religion', as I have noted there were even fewer Humanists than before and very few atheists. Given the dominance of secular propaganda and the surprising ways in which the Church of England has engineered its own demise, as this book has demonstrated, it is astonishing that nearly half the population still claims Christian allegiance. The world is ours to win for Christ and current circumstances demand more and not less of the distinctively *integral* mission and care that a parish system alone can offer.

If the parish did not exist, we would have to invent it.

Conclusion: *The Future Parish*

In this conclusion, I am going to try to be hopeful, despite everything that the Church of England is doing that makes me weep. We are all woefully in need of this theological virtue of hope in our dark days of the 2020s. I have already argued that we have the money, if we redirected resources, to provide more clergy and to train them effectively for parish ministry. A renewed attention to what I would call 'Deep Anglicanism' and more manageable jobs would make the priesthood more attractive to young people than it is at present. There is good evidence that traditional ministry performed with energy and imagination can succeed and generation Z, feeling deprived of family and community, is more receptive to faith than the generation before them. The world is all before us.

As I look around some of the parishes of the Church of England, I am filled with hope, because I see faithful ordinary Christians loving God and their neighbour and acting with the future in mind. At the end of Tom Holland's study of how Christianity made the ethical and cultural world we live in, he describes his own godmother:

> The story of how Christianity transformed the world, would never have happened without people like my Aunty Deb. A committed and faithful member of the Church of England, she took her duties as my godmother with the utmost seriousness. Having vowed at my baptism to see that I was brought up in the Christian faith and life, she did her best to keep her word ... Above all, through her unfailing kindness, she provided me with a model of what, to a committed Christian, the daily practice of her faith could actually mean.[1]

So long as there are parishioners like this, and I know of many, the Church will live.

I am also hopeful because of the nature of the crisis in which we find ourselves globally, in which neoliberalism is failing and fading either into a new totalitarianism or into an often atavistic populism. It is proving harder and harder to ground reality without the divine. This makes the need for a non-nationalist, non-racist thick but universal account of humanity all the more pressing and this, of course, is to be found in the Church as the place of reconciliation and witness to the possibility of a Common Good. There are parallels here with the situation following World War II with which I began this book, when totalitarian regimes had been destroyed and people looked for a good universal in which we might all share. The sociality of the Church and her call to co-operation and reconciliation spoke to the moment.

The New Synergy Between Parish and Society

Paul Avis has argued that society and churches rise and fall together: 'The relation between society and church is actually reciprocal. Their destinies are linked together. The Christian community and the wider community are in the same boat.'[2] Today our various national institutions are fragile and threatened, just as the Church is. So, what will enable the parish church to thrive in the future at this time of vulnerable institutions?

I noted in Chapter 2 that part of the success of the 1950s was that there was a synergy between the common-good communitarian and plurally corporatist politics of the time and the Church's own mission. We have the gift of a similar situation potentially emergent in our own era with the climate crisis, which has focused Church attention on its core theology of creation and also made us aware of the whole narrative of salvation as having an ecological dimension. Unlike the case of the embrace of theological liberalism in the 1960s, in which the world set the agenda and the Church internalized secular values, the new ecological attention chimes with the pan-sacramentality of so much Anglican theology over the centuries from the Cambridge Platonists, poets like Henry Vaughan and Christopher Smart, to the Anglican Distributist and early ecologist H. J. Massingham.[3]

As we saw in the last chapter, our parson naturalists always saw the parish as including all the forms of life within their care. This realization is increasingly energizing parishes up and down the country and is not an imposition from without. Whether there is a climate crisis or not, a theology of creation is central to Christian faith and its apologetic task. As I have argued, it is not just a question of presenting the good news of Christ today but of beginning further back and offering a proposal that the world has a divine origin and can be regarded as an infinitely crafted thing: as a divine gift.

Nowadays, ecological thinking has become the implicit 'faith' of the wider community, especially our secular education system, and is a common concern of everyone, as climate change produces such evident changes in our hot summers and frequent floods. The future parish will find a natural role through its gathering function as a site where we can make common cause to save our planet. Here is an example from Baroness Sherlock as she describes, in a Lords debate on the importance of the parish church, the Ecofest in her home parish of St John's Neville Cross in County Durham:

> The result is a huge mix of campaign groups, green campaigners, alternative energy providers, people who do vegetable boxes, beekeepers, fair trade stalls, bicycle repair workshops and a car-sharing club. There is also a toy swap-shop for the kids ... The Durham Foodbank will be there because many of our church members are involved in running it. At the end, our rector, Barney Huish, will lead us all in beer and hymns accompanied by a brass band, this being the north-east.[4]

Note how such an event allows worship and the proclamation of the gospel through hymn-singing, the nurturing of community as well as loving service, righting injustice and caring for creation: all the five marks of mission. The local church collaborates with other bodies involved in cognate activities, but through the gathering role that Oliver O'Donovan articulated as its key contribution. It joins in with foodbank and other community activities and does not try to do everything for itself, or even to lead.

Indeed, as the Common Good Foundation reminded us, poverty or vulnerability can become the occasion for new local relationships, as was the case for the new St John the Baptist Church on the Ermine estate at Lincoln. They could not afford grass cutting for the large area of open lawn around the church, so worked with the Lincoln Conservation Group to manage the site. The grass is allowed to grow, allowing wildflowers to thrive and volunteers come and scythe the area in hay season by hand.

This reliance on another body is a salutary example of how a future local church will learn to be humbler and to ask for help, seeing vulnerability as an opening to new relationships and mutual support. St Paul gives us an example in 1 Corinthians 2: 'I came to you in weakness and in fear and with much trembling.' The adjective 'humbler' in the *Vision and Strategy* strapline is rather code for pastoral reorganization and seems to offer little vision of this mutuality. We are beginning to understand our parochialism more humbly as a form of stewardship, rather than ownership. The formation of the National Trust and the nascent conservation bodies of the late nineteenth century came about through a new understanding of the land as not ours to do what we like with, in which we began to recover the medieval natural law approach, represented by Aquinas, for which any ownership was not absolute but held as stewardship of God's Providence.

In the Edwardian period, this idea of stewardship not absolute ownership was embodied in mediating spiritual figures, such as 'Lob' in a poem by Edward Thomas, one of the 'lords of No Man's Land', both as a figure for the common soldier sent to die for England throughout the centuries, and also of an idea of the land as a common inheritance, belonging to no one, with open paths.[5] We are of the earth, earthy, as 1 Corinthians 15.47 reminds us, but the earth is the Lord's. The spiritualizing of the landscape in the Edwardian period was a way of allowing place to be seen as enchanted and a gift.

The whole parish should have this character. Arwen Folkes suggests that we need 'a national campaign of re-enchantment. "This is your parish. Did you know? Weddings, baptisms, funerals, someone to talk to, questions about life ... We are here for you."'[6] She had in mind a Christmas advertisement and someone must have been listening because in December 2022 the Church of England did produce a well-thought-out Christmas video in which a child grows up and is welcomed at Christmas to different parish churches throughout her life, including being supported in her widowhood.[7] It was indeed, an enchanting story, but one that will ring hollow if the local churches are no longer there to welcome people.

The power of this video came from its personal character and the human friendship within the sacred places, for parish is the place where we find ourselves. Its local scale, which eco-theologian Michael Northcott defines as that of 'face-to-face communion, exchange and relations between persons, and between species' allows us to orient ourselves; it is where we start from and without that specific set of coordinates we cannot move or understand where we are, whether in a city, suburb or rural area.[8] It is the opposite of the tyrannical organization of space represented by the panopticon, as designed by the Utilitarian philosopher Jeremy Bentham, and which became such a feature of Michel Foucault's analysis of centralizing power. Bentham envisaged a prison in which one single guard could keep the whole building under surveillance and it has become a potent image for a scopophilic controlling gaze, which seeks to control and objectify that which it looks upon.[9] A true ecological parochialism is instead embedded in its community and sees itself as part of the wider habitat, constituted indeed by those relationships, which are all open to God. This is the genuine mixed ecology in which the relation is one of mutual support and interdependence, which Church of England documents may refer to but then betray by instituting policies of segregation and competition.

I have suggested that a key distinctive role of the parish worshipping community in its local ecology is one of gathering, having the building to enable the bringing together of different community groups; a second role appropriate to establishment is that of representation. Just as the late Queen Elizabeth in a speech at Lambeth Palace in 2012 described the role of the established church as one of advocacy for all faith traditions: 'The Church has a duty to protect the free practice of all faiths in this country', so this is true at the local level as well and not just in relation to those of other faiths, but in relation to the whole parish: plants, stones and creatures.[10] George Herbert describes the representative role of the human in his poem 'Providence':

> Man is the world's high Priest: he doth present
> The sacrifice for all; while they below
> Unto the service mutter an assent,
> Such as springs use that fall, and winds that blow.[11]

Humankind here mediates and offers praise on behalf of the whole natural order, which is seen to respond through being itself: its life is its prayer. He goes on to write that we 'rob a thousand' natural forms of their worship if we do not pray![12] A parish church is the ecclesial outworking of this priestly action, and it is exhibited in its activities but also in its intercessory prayer.

In the time of the Commonwealth in the seventeenth century, the poet Henry Vaughan, with Anglican liturgy proscribed, looked to the natural world to offer the liturgy that was lacking from humankind. In his poem 'The Bird' he goes further than Herbert in acknowledging the forms of the natural world as co-worshippers:

> All things that be, praise him, and had
> Their lesson taught them, when first made.
> So hills and valleys into singing break,
> And though poor stones have neither speech nor tongue,
> While active winds and streams both run and speak,
> Yet stones are deep in admiration.
> Thus Praise and Prayer here beneath the Sun
> Make lesser mornings, when the great are done.[13]

This goes much further than Common Worship Eucharistic Prayer G, where 'all your works echo the silent music of your praise'. In Vaughan some natural forms are speaking and even the silent stones are active in contemplation. They are not echoing anyone else's silent praise. Poetry, from *The Dream of the Rood* to the many religious poets of nature today, such as Peter Larkin and Abigail Carroll, offers some of our best eco-theology and it has the merit of being approachable for everyone. I spoke in an earlier chapter of the reviving study of Christian art, music and poetry in our schools, and our rich eco-theological tradition is one easy mode of entry.

The Future is Local

It is pointless, however, for the Church of England to embrace an ecologically sustainable future and at the same time plan ever larger ecclesial units, which will make clergy travel much further to the churches across the large area of the mission community or megaparish. As has been mentioned, such huge units will discriminate against the poor and the elderly laity, who are dependent on public transport, which is rarely available in the country on Sundays.

In the alternative future of the future parish (which I believe will prevail) in contrast to the current centralizing moves in some dioceses, which would condemn clergy to a life of constant commuting, the parish priest will not be a controller, rushing about unseen in a car but humbler, going about by cycle or on foot, or on the bus whenever practicable. I know one priest in London who uses one of those little electric scooters, which gives her both speed and an ability to be flagged down easily for conversation. I have myself never driven and find the different pace of public transport options and the psycho-geographical challenge of planning journeys never envisaged by bus-operators a real gift, which makes me experience places more intimately and surprisingly. While it might take me much longer than a car driver to reach somewhere, I can work on the bus or train, say my daily office or observe my fellow passengers, even having conversations with them. I never travel through empty space but through inhabited and embodied places.

This is the preamble to describing the second feature of the future parish, which is that it will be local in scale, enabling a local ministry on foot or cycle. Father Darren Percival walked the streets of his two deprived Leeds parishes, St Hilda's Cross Green and St Saviour's Richmond Hill, during Covid. He told the *Yorkshire Post*: 'It was important that people knew that though the building was closed, the church was still "open". I walked the streets of the two parishes in a cassock as usual, so people could see the church was still there for them.'[14] His many parochial activities during lockdown included a food-hub at St Hilda's, getting children involved in sporting challenges at home, and delivering Easter eggs to any child who put a drawing of one in their window. He did pastoral work sitting on a handy wall and his funeral ministry increased.

Similarly, during lockdown, Michelle Webb walked the streets of her estate parishes, St John's and St Giles' Lincoln, looking for families who would like a bag of biblical craft materials to replace the holiday club the parishes used to run. She found a door-step ministry as the bags provoked questions and curiosity about faith. By the end they were giving out 170 bags. This pastoral perambulation led to much listening, which enabled the churches to respond to evident food poverty with 'Free Tea Fridays' in the school holidays, offering a free meal, a biblical theme, a family challenge – such as making a bride's dress out of newspaper – and the opportunity to ask questions and offer prayer. When the donations ran out, miraculously businesses and local supermarkets stepped in to keep Free Tea Fridays going. Such activities gather community and proclaim the gospel.

As well as having enormous benefits in terms of really engaging with the parish, the move towards sustainable transport will have significant benefits in terms of clergy health, as they walk or cycle more. It will also assist clerical mental health because as a non-driver I have endured some appalling driving in lifts kindly offered by other clerics, who drive too fast, too aggressively and too close to cars in front – all I believe because of a sense of stress and (perceived) urgency. And it will aid mission, for the ministry of presence is incalculable in its effects. I go to my local street market on Saturday mornings and once counted the number of conversations I had, some with congregation members, others with stallholders or just other shoppers in the fish queue. It came to twelve, in under an hour, and that is a typical number, even though some of the chats are quite substantial and give me important information about who has had a fall, moved house or is just struggling, as well as establishing points of contact with people I have never met.

While this ministry of presence is ancient horse sense, it also belongs to the future, as other institutions see the benefit of being locally 'based' in both the older and the newer sense of the word. Daniel Finkelstein, writing in the *Times*, came to question his assumptions about economic growth and mobility in response to the very long-established Harvard Study of Human Development:

> Should the country try to move jobs to people or people to jobs? The free-market solution – the Norman Tebbit position, as it were – is that people should get on their bikes and look for work. There is no point trying to preserve declining areas. People should be encouraged to move somewhere that is doing better. The Harvard study immediately suggests that, for all the difficulties of a policy of levelling up, there is a strong argument for trying to move jobs to people. A 'place-based' approach to policy that seeks to revive areas where people already live seeks to preserve human connections.[15]

The 'get in your car' approach to parish amalgamations will similarly destroy the local connections that sustain community and human flourishing. Finkelstein realizes that this survey demonstrates why having a religious faith and practice renders people happier.

The police force has also realized the central importance of locality. Revd Dr Alan Billings is now Police and Crime Commissioner for South Yorkshire and in a recent article made comparisons between policing and church policy on visible presence. When the police force moved away from police on the beat in favour of mobile teams to save money, they found low-level criminality rising and public trust ebbing away. As the police are unarmed and rely on public consent, this was serious, and the policy was reversed, with neighbourhood teams now restored or established as policy for the future.[16] Billings sees an analogy with the move away from the local parish to mission hubs and the promotion of variant ecclesiologies, with a parallel alternative system promoted by the Anglican hierarchy. The parish model, like neighbourhood policing,

> … is also well understood and often supported by those who are not churchgoers. The vocabulary that we use – vicar, rector, curate, parish, parish church – has meaning for those who do not belong. It is this shared understanding, built up over generations, that allows the vicar to knock on a door, or call in at the local school or police station, without being invited. This operating model, with its neighbourhood focus, is what the police moved away from and had to recover.[17]

From his police experience he also calls out the impossibility of running two systems: 'it is quite disingenuous to say there will be a "mixed economy" or "mixed ecology". No organization can operate two operating models simultaneously without distorting its shape. It is a recipe for confusion and incoherence – which is already happening. (My chief constable asked me whether an oversight minister was a vicar.)'[18] The future parish will still be rooted in its neighbourhood and the clergy spend time propping up the bar in local hostelries and visiting cafes.

A second way in which society is in sync with the parish is the increasing turn to the local in politics and economics. There are massive pressures in the NHS for example, now in full-scale crisis, which are the result of too little agency at the local level, while the British Labour party is not alone in seeking policies of regional and local delegation and empowerment. In the United States, Bill Katz and Jeremy Nowak have written a book about what they call 'the new localism' in urban projects and economics. The Citizens movement and its model of community organizing is gaining traction throughout Britain and was addressed by all major prime ministerial candidates before the last general election. Many parishes, in cities particularly, have become involved in Citizens campaigns. Increasingly it is thought that our formal democracy needs to be supplemented by more informal and yet perhaps more genuinely represent-ative 'citizen assemblies' that often prove better at arriving at non-partisan solutions.

Since lockdown, home working has become ever more a reality for many employees and this tendency is set to increase, leading to increasing numbers of people choosing to move to rural areas to live and work. In the future, for a variety of reasons, we are more likely to live and work more locally with less commuting – even if the Church must absolutely not neglect those physical workers who still 'go to work', run greater risks and on whom we all rely. Already the high streets in small towns are becoming busier, if fuller of cafes and nice shops than before, while great shopping malls are eerily empty. This is therefore the worst time for the Church of England to be abandoning its rural heartlands, where 40% of its worshippers already live.

That does not mean that urban outreach should suffer. The Estates work sponsored by the Church of England, already mentioned, is a valuable form of outreach, based in the fifth of English parishes which have over 500 social housing units. In the three examples of estate parishes featured on podcasts pub-lished by the group, in dialogue with theologians, the churches in Wythenshawe, Rubery and Twydall were all deeply engaged with their community. Wythenshaw took the church out into the community by inviting people in various locations around the estate to contribute to a woven artwork of their experi-ence, blessings and struggles. Rubery, which is sliced by a dual carriageway, commissioned artists to work with local people on both sides of the divide in the no-man's-land under the A38 flyover to engender exciting community events in the space, while the inspiring Christians of Twydall offer the warmest of authentic welcomes at the heart of their estate. These communi-ties have churches on their estates, but half of all estate parishes have no building or worshipping community within the area of social housing, so that the need for pioneering outreach to draw people together is great. I pray and hope, however, that outreach in the future will be launched from the people in the parish, as is already often the case already, and not imposed by Bishop's Mission Order in such a way that it has no relation to the rest of the parish. Since community-building and listening is so central to this work, it would seem foreign to its nature to act in such a way.

Intensity, Intention and Imagination

I have noticed that successful clergy give an impression of a kind of thoughtfulness and communicativeness in their actions, whether it is shaking hands at the church door, presiding at the Eucharist or washing-up after a community meal. It is not exactly personal charisma, or extraversion (though the extraversion of some is crucial) but a kind of integrity and relaxation even, which comes from consciously inhabiting and performing a living way of life. You can see it also in lay people who are comfortable but alert in their role. When we are a shrinking body, this awareness of being part of a greater story allows a longer view, a sharper awareness of our purpose.

The future parish will have an intentional edge to all its activities, otherwise it will not survive. It will need to have loving relationships at its worshipping heart with what Dan Hardy called an 'intensity of participation in the new life of Christ', so that there is an urgency and sense of purpose in its core activities. Rootedness in history helps to form part of that intentionality, as people understand where they come from and thereby how they might contribute to the ongoing story of the church in that place. Hardy's stress on the importance of intensity, of living life as a parish with as strong relationships of trust as possible is accompanied with hospitality and an outward focus, and a concomitant parochial sense of 'extension of its benefit' beyond itself.[19] Congregations will need to be challenged to be outward looking, but this can only come from a proper local ministry where the priest is known and trusted.

The parish, as for an ecological theology, has to be seen as the whole area, and all its inhabitants, not just the worshipping community. If it is to gather, it needs to find occasions to discover what work God is already doing in the lives of people beyond its doors and honour it, as is already the case in the estates church examples. In the Rubery podcast from the Church of England Estates project, we heard the moving stories of two young single mothers, one with a particularly sad history of a controlling husband and addiction, who are obviously supporting each other with real devotion, and who found themselves listened to and valued at the church's community café. They are now enthusiastic supporters of family worship at the church and the vicar is to be godmother to the child of one of them.

In the estate examples of good news, art events and projects were at the heart of outreach and community representation. From my academic work on theology and the arts, I know how central the imagination is to an effective proposal of Christian truth and to empowering human beings to see themselves as gifted, made in the image of God the creator to share in some small way in his creative activity. The charity Art+Christianity works all over the country to accompany parishes in this work, whether it is commissioning new art, mounting exhibitions in churches or working with them to make art themselves. The collective Fourthland, for example, worked recently with women at St Andrew's Leytonstone and the local Hindu temple to explore ideas of sacred journeys and sanctuary, crafting artworks for each place of worship and a soundscape based on the women's memories. This art invoked Christian and Hindu rituals, but there are multiple ways in which churches can offer events that are purely artistic or literary in character such as concerts, plays or poetry readings, but also add a poetic edge to liturgy or offer a drama instead of a sermon. The visual arts have become much wider in appeal, especially in the form of monumental sculptures, and cathedrals find they can attract large audiences for impressive installations or works that fire the public imagination like the 'Knife Angel' crafted by Alfie Bradley made of weapons handed-in in response to the many police amnesties up and down the country.

There are also imaginative acts, which might not be regarded as art but in some sense are such. A parish in Withington, Lichfield Diocese sent a large lit-up star, mounted on a car, to a different location in the parish every night during Advent. Local people loved it and the village Whatsapp group was full of posts tracking its movements. The intense interest was reflected in the numbers at the 'Follow the Star' carol service. Was it an artwork? It was certainly a brilliant and imaginative intervention.

Future outreach will, I believe, increasingly be expressed through such creative modes and the parish church, which is already an artwork in itself, is an ideal home for this sort of activity. I am always astonished at how the most unlikely people will produce a passage that speaks to them when invited to bring a reading or image to speak to, and this kind of com- munal sharing can be very powerful. Any poet will tell you that you need a form to follow to allow a release of creativity and the parish is itself a form of life – what Dan Hardy called a 'socio-poesis' – which should encourage participation and creativity.[20] Hardy had in mind the parish generating ever expanding orders of relation, but the use of *poesis* or making suggests the making of some object.

One comparable institution to the parish is the local pub. In the recent Save the Parish Christmas stories, relations between parish church and pub were often close. In one parish, they took carols to the pub as a way of establishing wider links. So popu- lar was this venture, those attending outgrew the pub, so it now happens back in church, but with a pop-up bar run by the inn- keeper. Pubs too are under threat of closure, as people abandon public sociality, or just lack money; however, no one suggests they have 'failed' or are outdated as is the default position of the church hierarchy in relation to the parish. Their value is obvious to ordinary people, as is the parish to those outside the Church. The House of Lords debate at which Baroness Sher- lock spoke so powerfully about her parish ecofest was rich in speeches by peers of varied backgrounds and faiths about the social importance of the parish church.

Malcolm Guite suggests a synergy between CAMRA pub and parish in relation to mission and locality:

Not for the first time, I began to fantasize about founding CAMRE, the Campaign for Real Evangelism. Eschewing identikit evangelistic courses and formulae, or fizzy American imports, CAMRE would revive living local traditions, each as distinct as a local ale but each carrying the active ferment of the gospel; stirring and refreshing good news ...

Perhaps we should see each small parish as a kind of micro-brewery, combining an ancient recipe with local ingredients for a lively, distinct, and refreshing gift to its own community.

And maybe CAMRE could be as welcoming as CAMRA to the thirsty newcomer who has so much to learn and to savour.[21]

Each parish offers a specifically local brew, but like a true CAMRA pub is open to the wide variety of other local ales, just as anyone is welcome to come in.

Like the pub, the parish has been a constantly reshaped form of life over hundreds of years and its staying power is in that adaptability. In different ways, it has always kept the balance between the intensivity of a deep community life within its liturgical community and an outward-facing generosity towards its whole parish. R. S. Thomas described himself in a poem as a 'vicar of large things / in a small parish' and this is a vocation to which all parishioners are called: to find the eternal and the universal – large things – within the local and particular.[22] If the Church goes down the road of closing and amalgamating parish churches, she will find it ever more difficult to attend to small things and the needs of ordinary people. The parish priest, the outsider/insider, must hold the universal within the particular for his or her congregation, who are not, as Thomas admitted, 'small-minded', since indeed each person opens onto an infinite mystery.

Above all, the parish offers an opening to time, space and eternity: it is like the Tardis in that respect, much larger inside than out. I dedicated this book to two parish priests: John Suddards, who kept a light in his window to show parishioners he was there when they needed him, and David Scott, the gentle priest poet of Winchester, who supported For the Parish and spent many years in a single parish. He wrote a celebrated poem about our clerical working garment, the surplice, which speaks to his fellow priest-poet Malcolm Guite about the spiritual and poetic traditions he inhabits. It speaks to me similarly of the parish tradition that we live inside like an old cardigan:

> We have put these garments on
>   for centuries.
> They persist. We wither and
>   crease inside them.[23]

Like the surplice, the parish is a mode of life that we have inhabited for centuries, and like vestments, the parish and its practices of love, commitment and mutual support persist and outlast generations. May we continue to wear these Christ-like garments. And may the creativity and commitment of our parishes persist with new generations eager to carry on the tradition of a parish church for everyone. May the Church of England, which is nothing on earth but all her parishes and people, thereby flourish.

Notes

Introduction: For the Parish Twelve Years On

1 Brian Ferguson, 2020, 'Peter Howson: The Artist Inspired by Catastrophe He Saw Coming', *The Scotsman*, 17 May, at https://www.scotsman.com/arts-and-culture/art/peter-howson-artist-inspired-by-catastrophe-he-saw-coming-2855764 (accessed 28.4.23).

2 Quoted in Ferguson, 'Peter Howson'.

3 Andrew Davison and Alison Milbank, 2010, *For the Parish: A Critique of Fresh Expressions*, London: SCM Press.

4 Church of England, 2022, *Independent Report of Lowest Income Communities Funding and Strategic Funding*, at https://www.churchofengland.org/sites/default/files/2022-03/IRLS%20-%20final%20report%20%282%29.pdf (accessed 28.4.23).

5 Church of England, 2021, *Mission in Revision: A Review of the Mission and Pastoral Measure 2011*, at https://www.churchofengland.org/sites/default/files/2021-06/GS%202022%20-%20Mission%20in%20Revision%20-%20A%20Review%20of%20the%20Mission%20and%20Pastoral%20Measure%202011.pdf (accessed 28.4.23).

6 Madeleine Davies, 2021, 'Synod to Discuss 10,000 Lay-led Churches in the Next Ten Years', *Church Times*, 2 July, at https://www.churchtimes.co.uk/articles/2021/2-july/news/uk/synod-to-discuss-target-of-10-000-new-lay-led-churches-in-the-next-ten-years (accessed 28.4.23).

7 Martyn Percy, 2021, 'The Great Leap Forward Part One: The New Politics of Ecclesionomics for the Church of England', at https://modernchurch.org.uk/martyn-percy-the-great-leap-forward-part-one-the-new-politics-of-ecclesionomics-for-the-church-of-england (accessed 28.4.23).

8 Church of England, 2021, *Vision and Strategy*, at https://www.churchofengland.org/about/leadership-and-governance/emerging-church-england/vision-and-strategy (accessed 28.4.23).

9 I was prompted in choosing this title by that of a conference in which I participated under this title. The organisers were not so much thinking of King Arthur as Loren B. Mead's 1991 study, *The Once and Future Church: Reinventing the Congregation for a new Mission Frontier*, New York: Alban Institute.

NOTES

Chapter 1: National Mission and Local Embodiment

1 Jeremy Morris, 2022, *A People's Church: A History of the Church of England*, London: Profile.

2 Morris, *People's Church*, p. ix.

3 Morris, *People's Church*, p. 14.

4 William Cobbett, 1802, quoted in Jeremy Gregory and Jeffrey Scott Chamberlain (eds), *The National Church in Local Perspective*, Woodbridge: Boydell Press, 2003, p. 1.

5 See Karl Baus, Hans-Georg Becke, Eugen Ewig and Josef Vogt (eds), 1980, *The Imperial Church from Constantine to the Early Middle Ages*, London: Burns and Oates, pp. 230ff.

6 Nicholas Orme, 2021, *Going to Church in Medieval England*, New Haven CT: Yale, p. 23.

7 Andrew Rumsey, 2017, *Parish: An Anglican Theology of Place*, London: SCM Press, p. 101.

8 John Foxe, 1841 [1583], *Acts and Monuments*, ed. G. Townsend and S. R. Cattley, 8 vols, London: R. B. Seeley and W. Burnside, 1, pp. 519–20.

9 Richard Hooker, 1845 [1597], *Laws of Ecclesiastical Polity*, 2 vols, Oxford: Oxford University Press, III, I, 3, p. 277.

10 Hooker, *Laws*, V, lvi, 11, p. 630.

11 Paul Anthony Dominiack, 2020, *Richard Hooker: The Architecture of Participation*, London: T & T Clark.

12 This disjunction is both avoided and warned against in Clare Watkins, 2020, *Disclosing Church: An Ecclesiology Learned From Conversations in Practice*, London: Routledge, pp. 3–5.

13 I am indebted here to Jeremy Morris, *F. D. Maurice and the Crisis of Christian Authority*, Oxford: Oxford University Press, 2008, pp. 180–1. Hooker also employs the two natures of Christ to understand the mode of participation of the Church in the divine life. See *Laws*, V, liv, 5. p. 611.

14 *Life* quoted in Morris, *F. D. Maurice*, p. 178.

15 Peter Nockles, 1994, *The Oxford Movement in Context: Anglican High Churchmanship 1760–1857*, Cambridge: Cambridge University Press, pp. 149–51.

16 H. C. G. Moule, 1892, *Charles Simeon*, London: Methuen & Co, p. 29.

17 Elisabeth Jay, 1979, *The Religion of the Heart: Anglican Evangelicalism and the Nineteenth Century Novel*, Oxford: Clarendon Press, pp. 108, 112.

18 A. W. Brown, 1863, *Recollections of the Conversation Parties of the Rev Charles Simeon*, London: Hamilton, Adams and Co, p. 221.

19 S. A. Skinner, 2004, *Tractarians and the Condition of England:*

The Social and Political Thought of the Oxford Movement, Oxford: Clarendon Press, p. 139.

20 Skinner, *Tractarians*, p. 181.

21 Skinner, *Tractarians*, p. 146.

22 From T. Mozley, *Reminiscences* (1882), quoted in Skinner, *Tractarians*, p. 47.

23 Brewitt-Taylor, *Christian Radicalism*, pp. 90–1.

24 Joshua Penduck, 2017, 'The Week Evangelicals Began to Take Over the Church of England', 6 March, at https://openevangelical. wordpress.com/2017/03/06/the-week-evangelicals-began-to-take-over-the-church-of-england/ (accessed 28.4.23).

25 Justin Lewis-Anthony, 2009, *If You Meet George Herbert On the Road, Kill Him: Radically Rethinking Priestly Ministry*, London: Mowbray.

26 Christopher Ramsay, 1995, 'Nineteenth Century Urbanization and the Church of England: An Assessment', at www.Anglicanism.org (accessed 21.1.2023).

27 *Fresh Expressions in the Mission of the Church: Report of an Anglican-Methodist Working Party*, 2012, London: Church House, p. 76.

28 Thomas A. Robinson, 2016, *Who Were the First Christians? Dismantling the Urban Thesis*, Oxford: Oxford University Press.

29 John Hull, 2006, *Mission-shaped Church: A Theological Response*, London: SCM Press, p. 5.

30 Hull, quoted in *Fresh Expressions in the Mission of the Church*, p. 118.

31 *Mission-Shaped Church*, p. vii.

32 Abi Thompson, 'A Little World made Cunningly: In Defence of the Parish', *Church Times*, 15 September 2017 at https://www.churchtimes. co.uk/articles/2017/15-september/features/features/a-little-world-made-cunningly-in-defence-of-the-parish (accessed 28.4.23).

33 Thompson, 'Little World'.

Chapter 2: How Did We Get Here?

1 Alasdair MacIntyre, 1981, *After Virtue: A Study in Moral Theory*, London: Duckworth, p. 201.

2 C. S. Lewis, 2102 [1952], *Mere Christianity*, London: Collins, p. 28.

3 *Vision and Strategy*, 2021, at https://www.churchofengland.org/ about/leadership-and-governance/emerging-church-england/vision-and-strategy quoting the Archbishop of York, Stephen Cottrell (accessed 28.4.23).

4 William Temple, 1928, *Christianity and the State*, London: Macmillan, p. 170.

5 https://www.nationalarchives.gov.uk/cabinetpapers/alevelstudies/1951-conservative-management.htm (accessed 28.4.23).

6 Melville Dinwiddie, 1968, *Religion by Radio*, London: George Allen and Unwin, pp. 187–91.

7 Clive Field, 2015, *Britain's Last Religious Revival? Quantifying Belonging, Behaving, and Believing in the Long 1950s*, Basingstoke: Palgrave Macmillan, p. 59.

8 Field, *Britain's Last Religious Revival*, p. 25.

9 Andrew Brown and Linda Woodhead, 2016, *That Was the Church that Was: How the Church of England Lost the English People*, London: Bloomsbury, p. 68.

10 Tom Holland, 2019, *Dominion: The Making of the Western Mind*, London: Little Brown, p. 517.

11 Dietrich Bonhoeffer, 1963, *Letters and Papers from Prison*, London: Fontana, p. 123.

12 See Mark D. Chapman, 2006, 'Theology in the Public Arena: The Case of South Bank Religion', in *Redefining Christian Britain: Post 1945 Perspectives*, eds Jane Garnett, Matthew Grimley, Alana Harris, William Whyte and Sarah Williams, London: SCM Press, 2006, pp. 92–105 (pp. 92–3).

13 Chapman, 'Theology in the Public Arena', 93.

14 Chapman, 'Theology in the Public Arena', 94.

15 Geoffrey Hill, 1978, *Tenebrae*, London: Andre Deutsch, p. 41, https://www.trinitycollegebristol.ac.uk/blog/kingdom-learning/new-class-on-bonhoeffer/ (accessed 28.4.23).

16 John Robinson, 1974 [1963], *Honest to God*, London: SCM Press, p. 38.

17 Barry Hill, '2021, Why a Mixed Ecology Matters', *Church Times*, 21 November, at https://www.churchtimes.co.uk/articles/2021/12-november/comment/opinion/why-a-mixed-ecology-matters (accessed 28.4.23).

18 Robinson, *Honest to God*, p. 104.

19 Chapman, 'Theology in the Public Arena', p. 102.

20 Chapman, 'Theology in the Public Arena', p. 102.

21 Sam Brewitt-Taylor, 2018, *Christian Radicalism in the Church of England and the Invention of the British Sixties, 1957–1970*, Oxford: Oxford University Press.

22 Brewitt-Taylor, *Christian Radicalism*, p. 45.

23 Brewitt-Taylor, *Christian Radicalism*, p. 44.

24 Sean Lang, 2000, 'A-Level History', *History Today* 50, no. 2, at https://www.historytoday.com/archive/level-history (accessed 28.4.23).

25 Maurice Cowling, 1980, *Religion and Public Doctrine in Modern England*, Cambridge: Cambridge University Press.

26 Church of England, 1985, *Faith in the City: The Report of the Archbishops' Commission on Urban Priority Areas*, London: Church House, Chapter 3.

27 Andrew Hake, 1989, 'Theological Reflections on Community', in *Theology in the City: A Theological Response to 'Faith in the City'*, London: SPCK, pp. 50–2. It is worth recording, as I critique the theological language, that Hake had a distinguished practical involvement in shanty-town ministry.

28 Church of England, 2023, Baptism and Confirmation, at https://www.churchofengland.org/prayer-and-worship/worship-texts-and-resources/common-worship/christian-initiation/baptism-and#, p. 168 (accessed 28.4.23).

Chapter 3: Follow the Money

1 Response to Question 13 by Roy Faulkner at General Synod in November 2021. See https://www.churchofengland.org/sites/default/files/2021-11/question-13-page-1.pdf (accessed 25.8.23).

2 https://www.oxford.anglican.org/who-we-are/bishops-and-senior-staff/ (accessed 28.4.23).

3 Leslie Paul, 1964, *The Deployment and Payment of the Clergy*, London: Church Information Office, pp. 81–8.

4 Quoted in Peter Armstrong, *Team Ministries in Anglican Parishes in the Maritime Provinces of Canada: Considerations for Formation and Development*, Thesis submitted to the Faculty of Wycliffe College and the Toronto School of Theology, 2015, at https://tspace.library.utoronto.ca/bitstream/1807/69173/6/Armstrong_Peter_L_201505_DMin_thesis.pdf (accessed 28.4.23).

5 A. Tindal Hart, 'Is Saul [Paul] Also Among the Prophets? The Proposal to Transform Rural Deaneries into Major Parishes with a Team', *The Paul Report Considered: Thirteen Essays*, ed. G. E. Duffield, Oxford: Marcham Manor Press, 1964, p. 29.

6 Eric Treacy, 'Approaching the Report', *Paul Report Considered*, p. 10.

7 Monica Hewitt, 'A Sociological Critique', *Paul Report Considered*, p. 21.

8 Hewitt, 'A Sociological Critique', *Paul Report Considered*, p. 21.

9 F. R. Barry, 'Priorities', *Paul Report Considered*, p. 26.

10 Fiona Tweedie, 2016, *Going Deeper: Church Attendance Statistics and Clergy Deployment*, at https://www.churchofengland.org/sites/default/files/2020-01/going_deeper_final_0.pdf, p. 1 (accessed 28.4.23).

11 *From Anecdote to Evidence: Findings from the Church Growth Research Programme, 2011–2013*, at https://www.churchofengland.org/resources/church-growth-research-programme/anecdote-evidence (accessed 28.4.23).

12 Tiffer Robinson in *Anecdote to Evidence*, p. 16.

13 Diocese of Leicester, 2022, *Shaped By God: Frequently Asked Questions*, p. 2.

14 Leicester, *Frequently Asked Questions*, p. 3.

15 See Angela Tilby, 2021, 'Ministry that is Lay-led is not Anglican', *Church Times*, 8 October at https://www.churchtimes.co.uk/articles/2021/8-october/comment/columnists/angela-tilby-ministry-that-is-lay-led-is-not-anglican (accessed 28.4.23).

16 Madeleine Davies, 2021, 'Focal Oversight the Church of England of the Future', *Church Times*, 10 September, at https://www.churchtimes.co.uk/articles/2021/10-september/features/features/focal-oversight-the-c-of-e-of-the-future (accessed 28.4.23).

17 Liverpool Diocese, 2022, *Fit for Mission*, at https://liverpool.anglican.org/making-it-easier-parishes/fitformission/led-by-local-teams/ (accessed 28.4.23).

18 Representations by parishioners to the Church Commissioners, at www.churchofengland.org/sites/default/files/2019-08/Wigan%20-%20Representations%20-%20pages%20R201-R240.pdf (accessed 28.4.23).

19 All details taken from representations by parishioners to the Church Commissioners, at www.churchofengland.org/sites/default/files/2019-08/Wigan%20-%20Representations%20-%20pages%20R201-R240.pdf (accessed 28.4.23).

20 http://cinw.s3.amazonaws.com/wp-content/uploads/2013/08/Ministry-Areas-English-Text-on-line.pdf (accessed 28.4.23).

21 Para 35.

22 Clare Vickers et al, 2022, Letters, *Church Times*, 18 March, at https://www.churchtimes.co.uk/articles/2022/18-march/comment/letters-to-the-editor/letters-to-the-editor (accessed 28.4.23).

23 Church of England, 2021, *Mission in Revision: Review of the Mission and Pstoral Measure 2011*, at https://www.churchofengland.org/sites/default/files/2021-06/GS%202222%20-%20Mission%20in%20Revision%20-%20A%20Review%20of%20the%20Mission%20and%20Pastoral%20Measure%202011.pdf (accessed 28.4.23).

24 Anthony Jennings, 2022, 'The Long Fight to Protect the Parish', at https://savetheparish.com/2022/11/23/the-long-fight-to-protect-the-parish-anthony-jennings/ (accessed 28.4.23).

25 National Churches Trust, 2018, *Visiting Churches*, at https://www.nationalchurchestrust.org/news/49-cent-british-adults-visited-church-last-year (accessed 28.4.23).

26 Financial Scrutiny Group of Save the Parish, at https://savetheparish.com/church-of-england-finance/ (accessed 28.4.23).

27 Arthur Burns, 1999, *The Diocesan Revival in the Church of England*, Oxford: Oxford University Press, p. 189.

28 Kenneth Thompson, 1975, 'Church House and Margaret Parkes', *Astonishing Good Fortune*, Loughborough: West and Lissaman, p. 68.

29 Terence Walker MP, 1976, *Hansard* debate on Endowments and Glebe Measure, vol. 919, cols 941–6, 15 November, 1976 at https://hansard.parliament.uk/Commons/1976-11-15/debates/290098fd-cef7-4109-ae97-c3c6dfb44898/ChurchOfEngland(EndowMentsAnd GlebeMeasure) (accessed 28.4.23).

30 Chote Report, p. 27.

31 Chote Report, p. 27.

32 Chote Report, pp. 27–8.

33 Madeleine Davies, 2019, 'Revitalising Mission – but at What Cost?', *Church Times*, 22 November, at https://www.churchtimes.co.uk/articles/2019/22-november/features/features/revitalising-mission-but-at-what-cost (accessed 28.4.23).

34 See Southwell and Nottingham Petertide Ordinations, 2021, at https://southwell.anglican.org/petertide-ordinations-2021/ (accessed 28.4.23).

35 Chote Report, p. 6.

36 Sir James Burnell-Nugent, letter on 11 March 2022 in *Church Times*, which was commended by the leader writer at-in the same issue, at https://www.churchtimes.co.uk/articles/2022/11-march/comment/letters-to-the-editor/letters-to-the-editor (accessed 28.4.23).

37 Church of England, 2017, *Setting God's People Free*, p. 8.

38 James Noyes and Phillip Blond, *Holistic Mission*, London: ResPublica, 2013, p. 6.

39 Hannah Rich, 2020, *Growing Good: Growth, Social Action and Discipleship in the Church of England*, London: Theos, pp. 12–14, at https://cuf.org.uk/uploads/resources/CUF-GRACE-Report-2020.pdf (accessed 28.4.23).

40 Madeleine Davies, 2021, 'Synod to Discuss Target of 10,000 New-Laid Churches in the Next Ten Years', at https://www.churchtimes.co.uk/articles/2021/2-july/news/uk/synod-to-discuss-target-of-10-000-new-lay-led-churches-in-the-next-ten-years (accessed 28.4.23).

Chapter 4: Managerial Mission

1 Lyndon Shakespeare, 2016, *Being The Body of Christ in an Age of Management*, Eugene OR: Cascade, pp. 54–5.

2 Vanessa Elston, 2021, Diocese of Southwark, MAP Values, at southwark.anglican.org/wp-content/uploads/2021/02/MAP-values_F.pdf (accessed 28.4.23).

3 Justin Lewis-Anthony, 2019, 'A Gregorian Critique of managerialism', p. 17, at https://www.academia.edu/9890319/Ecclesiastical_Bureaucracy_a_Gregorian_critique_of_Managerialism (accessed 28.4.23).

4 Shakespeare, *Being the Body of Christ*, p. 39.

5 Stephen Pattison, 1997, *The Faith of the Managers*, New York: Continuum, p. 38.

6 Shakespeare, *Being the Body of Christ*, p. 52.

7 Straplines for dioceses of Rochester, Truro, Liverpool and St Edmundsbury and Ipswich.

8 Robert Putnam, 2001, *Bowling Alone: the Collapse and Revival of American Community*, New York: Simon and Schuster.

9 https://johnquiggin.com/2003/07/02/word-for-wednesday-managerialism-definition/ (accessed 28.4.23).

10 Martyn Percy, 2012, *The Ecclesial Canopy: Faith, Hope and Charity*, Farnham: Ashgate, p. 20.

11 MacIntyre, *After Virtue*, p. 175.

12 Shakespeare, *Being the Body of Christ*, p. 96.

13 Davison and Milbank, *For the Parish*, pp. 65–73, 75–81.

14 Karen Dale, 2001, *Anatomising Embodiment and Organization Theory*, Basingstoke: Palgrave, p. 21.

15 Remi Jardat, 2007, 'How Democratic Internal Law Leads to Low Cost Efficient Processes', *Society and Business Review* 3, no. 1, pp. 23–40 (p. 23).

16 Archbishop of York's Commentary on *Vision and Strategy*, at https://www.churchofengland.org/sites/default/files/2021-06/A%20vision%20for%20the%20church%20of%20England%20in%20the%202020s%20-%20commentary%20by%20Stephen_Cottrell.pdf, p. 2 (accessed 28.4.23).

17 MacIntyre, *After Virtue*, p. 194.

18 Diocese of Liverpool, 2022, *A Brief Guide to Pastoral Reorganisation*, at https://d3hgrlq6yacptf.cloudfront.net/603eb0893e402/content/pages/documents/pastoral_reorganisation_leaflet_v1.pdf , p. 1 (accessed 28.4.23).

19 Liverpool, *Guide to Pastoral Reorganisation*, p. 1.

20 East Wivelshire, On the Way Steering Group, 2022, 'Letter and Proposal of the East Wivelshire Steering Group, pdf', p. 1.

21 Church of England, 2022, *Governance Review Update*, para 19, 10, at https://www.churchofengland.org/sites/default/files/2022-06/GS%20Misc%201319%20Governance%20Review_0.pdf (accessed 28.4.23). https://hbr.org/2002/03/do-you-have-a-well-designed-organization (accessed 28.4.23).

22 *Governance Review Update*, para. 24, p. 10.

23 See Church of England, 2022, *A Consultation Document: Bishops and their Ministry Fit for a New Context*, at https://www.churchtimes.co.uk/articles/2022/18-february/news/uk/bishops-and-their-ministry-full-document, para 2.5.4 (accessed 28.4.23).

24 Darrell L. Guder and Lois Barrett, 1998, *Missional Church: A Vision for the Sending of the Church in North America*, Grand Rapids: Eerdmans, p. 37.

25 *Setting God's People Free: A Report of the Archbishops' Council*, at https://www.churchofengland.org/sites/default/files/2017-11/gs-20 56-setting-gods-people-free.pdf, pp. 1–2 (accessed 28.4.23).

26 *Setting God's People Free*, p. 5.

Chapter 5: The Parish Between Church Planting and Pioneer Ministry

1 Davison and Milbank, *For the Parish*, pp. 69, 73–5, 142.

2 Anderson Jeremiah, 2021, 'Mixed Ecology Church: Why Definitions Matter', *Church Times, 23 July, at* https://www.churchtimes.co.uk/articles/2021/23-july/comment/opinion/mixed-ecology-church-why-definitions-matter (accessed 28.4.23).

3 Tim Thorlby, 2016, *Love, Sweat and Tears: Church Growth in East London*, London: Centre for Theology and Community, p. 26.

4 Church Army, 2021, *Pioneering in Portsmouth*, p. 21.

5 Martyn Percy, 'Mega-churches'.

6 On its history and development see Andrew Atherstone, 2022, *Repackaging Christianity: Alpha and the Building of a Global Brand*, London: Hodder and Stoughton, 2022.

7 Rich Moy's thesis is published in a long series of blogposts, at https://yournameislikehoney.com/category/ministry/church-of-england-ministry/ (accessed 28.4.23).

8 Rich Moy, 2015, 'Men Only? A Charismatic Crisis in HTB/New Wine Leadership', at https://yournameislikehoney.com/2015/12/05/men-only-a-charismatic-crisis-in-new-wine-htb-leadership/ (accessed 28.4.23).

9 Canon B22 for Baptisms and B38 for funerals. B35, 1 on marriages refers to state law.

10 Rich Moy, 2022, 'In the Shadow of Success', at https://yourname islikehoney.com/2022/01/03/part-seventeen-in-the-shadow-of-success-5-questions-for-htb-network/ (accessed 28.4.23).

11 Madeleine Davies, 'Priests and Bishops a Given in Myriad's Vision for Lay-led Churches', *Church Times*, 30 July 2021, at https://www.churchtimes.co.uk/articles/2021/30-july/news/uk/priests-and-bishops-a-given-in-myriad-s-vision-for-lay-led-churches (accessed 28.4.23).

12 Madeleine Davies, 'Lay Church Planters Held Back by Church Structures', *Church Times*, 25 February, at https://www.churchtimes.co.uk/articles/2022/25-february/news/uk/lay-church-planters-held-back-by-church-structures-study-suggests (accessed 28.4.23).

13 John McGinley, 2022, *Listening to the Voice of the Lay Planters*, Centre for Church Multiplication, p. 25.

14 McGinley, *Voice of the Lay Planters*, pp. 22, 18.

15 McGinley, *Voice of the Lay Planters*, p. 23.

16 George Lings, *Encountering the Day of Small Things*, Sheffield: Church Army, 2017, p. 21.

17 Articles of Religion, 1968 [1662], *The Book of Common Prayer*, London: Eyre and Spottiswoode, p. 692.

18 Lings, *Encountering the Day*, p. 111.

19 Syke Community Church at the Antioch Network, Diocese of Manchester, formerly at https://www.antiochnetwork.org.uk/syke-community-church.

20 Vocations to Pioneer Ministry, 2023, at https://www.churchof england.org/life-events/vocations/vocations-pioneer-ministry (accessed 28.4.23).

21 Lings, *Encountering the Day*, p. 21.

22 Lings, *Encountering the Day*, p. 199.

23 Lings, *Encountering the Day*, p. 13.

24 Church Army, *Pioneering in Portsmouth*, pp. 9–10.

25 Church Army, *Pioneering in Portsmouth*, p. 10.

26 Martin Payne, 2015, 'A Year in the Life of One Messy Church', at https://www.messychurch.org.uk/messy-blog/year-life-one-messy-church (accessed 28.4.23).

27 Lings, *Encountering the Day*, p. 21.

Chapter 6: Bishops and Parishes: What is the Church?

1 Roman Catholic Church, 1983, Canon 368, *Code of Canon Law*, at https://www.vatican.va/archive/cod-iuris-canonici/eng/documents/cic_lib2-cann368-430_en.html#SECTION_II._PARTICULAR_CHURCHES_AND_THEIR_GROUPINGS (accessed 28.4.23).

2 Paul Avis, 2007, *The Identity of Anglicanism: Essentials of Anglican Ecclesiology*, London: T & T Clark, p. 167.

3 Ignatius of Antioch, 1996, *Epistle to the Ephesians*, Ante-Nicene Fathers 1, trans. Alexander Roberts and James Donaldson, rev. A. Cleveland Coxe, Edinburgh: T & T Clark, pp. 50–1.

4 Hooker, *Laws*, VII.II, 3, p. 34.

5 J. V. Bullard, 1938, *The English Parish and Diocese*, London: Faith Press, pp. 7–9.

6 Hooker, *Laws*, VII.II, 2, p. 34.

7 Angela Tilby, 2022, 'Bishops' Unanimity is Shameful', *Church Times*, 4 March, at https://www.churchtimes.co.uk/articles/2022/4-march/comment/columnists/angela-tilby-bishops-unanimity-is-shameful Cleveland Coxe, Edinburgh. She also refers to Evans's comments in the webinar, in which she too participated.

8 Avis, *Identity of Anglicanism*, p. 167.

9 Alex Blöchlinger, 1965, *The Modern Parish Community*, London: Geoffrey Chapman, pp. 3–37.

10 Church of England, 2023, *Canons of the Church of England*, Canon C18, at https://www.churchofengland.org/about/leadership-and-gov ernance/legal-services/canons-church-england/canons-website-edition (accessed 28.4.23).

11 Cyprian of Carthage, 1995, *On the Unity of the Church*, The *Ante-Nicene Fathers*, 5, eds Alexander Roberts and James Donaldson, rev. A. Cleveland Coxe, Edinburgh: T & T Clark, p. 423.

12 Quoted in Arthur Burns, 1999, *The Diocesan Revival in the Church of England*, Oxford: Oxford University Press, p. 93.

13 Raymond Ravenscroft, 2008, 'Role of the Rural Dean', *Ecclesiastical Law Journal* 5, no. 12, July 2008, pp. 42-45 (43).

14 Diocese of Exeter, 2015, *Handbook for Rural Deans 1.1, revised*, p. 2.

15 See Manchester and Birmingham: the latter diocese has added greatly to the number of its deans at the same time as it makes their role full-time.

16 Diocese of Manchester, 2021, Antioch Network, at https://www. manchester.anglican.org/antioch-network.php (accessed 28.4.23).

17 Ignatius of Antioch, 1995, *Epistle to the Trallians*, The *Ante-Nicene Fathers*, 1, eds Alexander Roberts and James Donaldson, rev. A. Cleveland Coxe, Edinburgh: T & T Clark, pp. 66–7.

18 Quoted in Rupert Bursell, 2014, 'The Oath of Canonical Obedience', *Ecclesiastical Law Journal* 16, pp. 168–86 (p. 170).

19 Church of England, Canon C14.

20 I am indebted to Angela Tilby for calling my attention to this change. Bursell asserts that there is no real difference between obedience and allegiance but this is unconvincing.

21 Church of England, 2021, *Governance Review Group Report*, at https://www.churchofengland.org/sites/default/files/2021-09/Govern ance%20Review%20Group%20Report%20FOR%20PUBLICATION. pdf (accessed 28.4.23).

22 *Governance Review Group Report*, p. 24.

23 John Neville Figgis, 1913, *Churches in the Modern State*, London: Longmans.

24 Rebecca Chapman, 'There is an Alternative to Vision and Strategy', *Church Times*, 18 November, at https://www.churchtimes.co.uk/ articles/2022/18-november/comment/opinion/there-is-an-alternative-to-vision-and-strategy (accessed 28.4.23).

25 Chapman, 'There is an Alternative.'

26 *Governance Review Group Report*, pp. 32–4.

27 *Governance Review Group Report*, p. 140.

28 Martyn Percy, '2022, Some Critical Comment on 'Bishops and Ministry Fit for a New Context', at https://anglican.ink/2022/02/21/ martyn-percy-some-critical-comment-on-bishops-and-ministry-fit-for-a-new-context/ (accessed 28.4.23).

29 'Hierarchy is a sacred order, knowledge and activity, which is being assimilated to likeness with God as much as possible.' Dionysius the Areopagite, 1987, *The Celestial Hierarchy, Pseudo-Dionysius: The Complete Works*, trans. Colm Luibheid, ed. Paul Rorem, London: SPCK, p. 153.

30 Colin Podmore, 2006, 'The Church of England's Understanding of Episcopacy', *Theology* 109, no. 849, pp. 173–81 (p. 177).

31 Ian Hart, 1995, 'The Teaching of Luther and Calvin about Ordinary Work: 1 Martin Luther (1483–1546)', *Evangelical Quarterly* 67, no. 1, pp.35–52 (p. 51).

32 See Common Awards Programme Specification for B.A. in Theology, Ministry and Mission, St Mellitus, at https://www.durham.ac. uk/media/durham-university/departments-/common-awards/docu ments/curriculum-programme-specifications/Prog_Spec_BA.pdf (accessed 28.4.23).

33 Oliver O'Donovan, 2005, *Ways of Judgment*, Grand Rapids MI: Eerdmans, p. 286.

34 O'Donovan, *Ways of Judgment*, pp. 288-9.

35 Martyn Percy, '1997, Consecrated Pragmatism', *Anvil* 14, no. 1, pp. 18-28 (p. 19).

36 Tom O'Loughlin, 2015, *Washing Feet: Imitating the Example of Jesus in the Liturgy Today*, Collegeville MN: Liturgical Press.

Chapter 7: The Crisis in Education and Communal Memory

1 Church of England, 2022, 'Church schools and academies', at https://www.churchofengland.org/about/education-and-schools/church-schools-and-academies (accessed 28.4.23).

2 Bible Society, 2014, *Pass It On*, at https://www.biblesociety.org. uk/uploads/content/projects/Bible-Society-Report_030214_final_.pdf (accessed 28.4.23).

3 MacIntyre, *After Virtue*, p. 201.

4 See the very positive report on the programme by Rachel Shillitoe, 2020, at https://www.understandingchristianity.org.uk/the-project/pro ject-evaluation-understanding-christianity/ , p. 14 (accessed 28.4.23).

5 Hawarang Moon, 2021, 'The Influence of Liturgy on Memory: From the Perspective of Neuroscience', *Studia Liturgica* 5, no. 2, pp. 230–42 (p. 232).

6 Hawarang Moon, 1998, 'Influence of Liturgy on Memory', 232, quoting Gordon Lathrop, *Holy Things: A Liturgical Theology*, Minneapolis, MN: Augsburg Fortress.

7 Martyn Percy, 2017, 'How George Bell Became a Victim of Church of England Spin and Decisive Leadership', Archbishop Cranmer Blog, 17 November, at https://archbishopcranmer.com/bishop-george-bell-

victim-church-england-spin-narrative-decisive-leadership/ (accessed 28.4.23).

8 I am taking these figures from Ian Paul's blog post, 2019, 'What Are the Issues in Ministerial Education', at https://www.psephizo. com/life-ministry/what-are-the-issues-in-ministerial-training/ (accessed 28.4.23). See also Church of England, 2015, *Resourcing Ministerial Education in the Church of England* at https://www.churchofengland. org/sites/default/files/2017-12/gs%201979%20-%20resourcing%20 ministerial%20education%20task%20group%20report.pdf (accessed 28.4.23).

9 Ian Paul, 2019, 'What Are the Issues in Ministerial Training, at https://www.psephizo.com/life-ministry/what-are-the-issues-in-minis terial-training/ (accessed 28.4.23).

10 See Alison Milbank, 2011, 'Apologetics and the Imagination: Making Strange', *in Imaginative Apologetics: Theology, Philosophy and the Catholic Tradition*, ed. Andrew Davison, London: SCM Press, pp. 31–45.

11 Simone Weil, 2008 [1949], *The Need for Roots: Prelude to a Declaration of Duties Towards Mankind*, trans Arthur Wills, London: Routledge, p. 51.

12 MacIntyre, *After Virtue*, p. 199.

13 MacIntyre, *After Virtue*, p. 225.

14 Tom Holland, 2019, *Dominion: The Making of the Western Mind*, London: Little, Brown.

15 Imogen Sinclair, 'How Generation Z Can Save the Conservative Party', *New Statesman* 14 July 2023.

Chapter 8: Kill the Parish?

1 See James Cameron, 2018, 'Black Metal Church Burnings: A Historical View', at https://stainedglassattitudes.wordpress.com/2018/01/13/ black-metal-church-burnings-a-historical-view/ (accessed 28.4.23).

2 Ian Paul, 2020, 'What is Happening to Church of England Attendance', at https://www.psephizo.com/life-ministry/what-is-happen ing-to-church-of-england-attendance/ (accessed 28.4.23).

3 Richard Giles, John Sadler and Robert Warren, 2020, 'Lockdown Could Change the Church Permanently', *Church Times*, 29 May, at https://www.churchtimes.co.uk/articles/2020/29-may/comment/opinion/ lockdown-could-change-the-church-permanently (accessed 28.4.23).

4 Paul Avis, 2003, *Church Drawing Near: Spirituality and Mission in a Post-Christian Culture*, London: T & T Clark, p. 197.

5 Avis, *Church Drawing Near*, 197.

6 Tiffer Robinson, 2022, ' Saving the Parish is Possible', at https://

saveteparish.com/2022/04/26/saving-the-parish-is-possible-rev-canon-tiffer-robinson/ (accessed 28.4.23).

7 Quoted in Madeleine Davies, 'The Love Affair with the Parish: Has it Ended?', at https://www.churchtimes.co.uk/articles/2021/17-september/features/features/the-love-affair-with-the-parish-has-it-ended (accessed 28.4.23).

8 Davies, 'Love Affair with the Parish'.

9 Davison and Milbank, *For the Parish*, pp. 144–69.

10 Carol Davidson Cragoe, 2010, 'The Custom of the English Church: Parish Church Maintenance in England before 1300', *Journal of Medieval History* 36, no. 1, pp. 20–38.

11 St Andrews Owston, 2022, 'Parishes at Christmas', at https://saveteparish.com/2022/12/21/parishes-at-christmas-various/ (accessed 28.4.23).

12 See the report by Nick Haynes, *Research Report on Church-State Relationships in Selected European Countries*, June 20028, at http://www.hrballiance.org.uk/wp-content/uploads/2015/01/church-state-relationships.pdf (accessed 28.4.23).

13 See National Churches Trust, 2021, *The House of Good*, p. 5.

14 See Church of England, 2021, 'Safeguarding: Learning and Development Framework', p. 5, at https://www.churchofengland.org/sites/default/files/2021-06/SafeguardingLearningAndDevelopmentFramework2021.pdf (accessed 28.4.23).

15 James Noyes and Phillip Blond, 2013, *Holistic Mission: Social Action and the Church of England*, Lincoln: ResPublica, p. 9.

16 Noyes and Blond, *Holistic Mission*, p. 1.

17 Noyes and Blond, *Holistic Mission*, p. 9, quoting Adam Dinham, 2008, 'Commentary: From Faith in the City to Faithful Cities: The "Third Way", the Church of England and Urban Regeneration', *Urban Studies* 40, no. 10, p. 2163.

18 Video at National Churches Trust, *House of Good*, at https://www.houseofgood.nationalchurchestrust.org (accessed 28.4.23).

19 Rumsey, *Parish*, pp. 164–5.

20 See Rumsey, *Parish*, p. 165.

21 See A Rocha, 'Stories', at https://ecochurch.arocha.org.uk/stories/ (accessed 28.4.23).

22 Autumn Newsletter of Parish Church Ministries, 2022 at https://parishnursing.org.uk/news/ (accessed 28.4.23).

23 Tim Thorlby, *A Time to Sow: Anglican Catholic Church Growth in London*, London: Centre for Theology and Community, 2017.

24 St George's in the East, 2023, 'Partnerships', at https://www.stgeorgeintheeast.org/partnerships (accessed 28.4.23).

25 Save the Parish, 'Parishes at Christmas'.

26 Weil, *The Need for Roots*, p. 52.

27 Church for Everyone, 2022, 'Enriched by the Farsi Community: Holy Innocents Fallowfield', at https://churchforeveryone.info/asylum-church-stories-holy-innocents (accessed 28.4.23).

28 Common Good Foundation, *The Plague and the Parish*, at https://togetherforthecommongood.co.uk/leading-thinkers/the-plague-and-the-parish (accessed 18.8.23).

29 https://www.vatican.va/content/benedict-xvi/en/speeches/2010/september/documents/hf_ben-xvi_spe_20100917_societa-civile.html (accessed 28.4.23).

Conclusion: *The Future Parish*

1 Holland, *Dominion*, pp. 517–18.

2 Avis, *Church Drawing Near*, p. 170.

3 H. J. Massingham, 2003 [1943], *The Tree of Life*, Intro. Frances Hutchinson, London: Jon Carpenter.

4 Baroness Sherlock, 2014, Hansard, 2014, HL Debate on the Importance of the English Parish Church, vol. 754, cols 542–78, 12 June, at https://hansard.parliament.uk/lords/2014-06-12/debates/1406 1242000654/EnglishParishChurches (accessed 28.4.23).

5 Edward Thomas, 1975, 'Lob', *Poems of Edward Thomas*, intro. Walter de la Mare, Oxford: Oxford University Press, p. 39.

6 Davies, *Love Affair*.

7 Church of England, 2022, 'Follow the Star: The Great Invitation', at https://www.churchofengland.org/media-and-news/press-releases/christmas-film-2022 (accessed 28.4.23).

8 Michael Northcott, 2011, 'Parochial Ecology on St Briavels Common: Rebalancing the Local and the Universal in Anglican Ecclesiology and Practice', *Journal of Anglican Studies* 10, no. 1, pp. 68–93 (p. 73).

9 Michel Foucault, 1977, *Discipline and Punish: The Birth of the Prison*, trans. Alan Sheridan, Harmondsworth: Penguin, pp. 195–228.

10 Queen Elizabeth II, 'Speech at Lambeth Palace, 5 February 2012', at https://www.royal.uk/queens-speech-lambeth-palace-15-february-2012 (accessed 28.4.23). 2023.

11 George Herbert, 1991, 'Providence', *The Complete English Poems*, ed. John Tobin, London: Penguin, pp. 108–13 (p. 109).

12 Herbert, *Complete English Poems*, p. 109.

13 Henry Vaughan, 1914, 'The Bird', *The Works of Henry Vaughan*, 2 vols, ed. Leonard Cyril Martin, Oxford: Clarendon Press, 2, pp. 496–7.

14 Felicity McCormick, 2022, 'Father Darren Percival BEM: Yorkshire vicar who serves one of the poorest parishes in the country honoured', *Yorkshire Post*, 2 June, at https://www.yorkshirepost.co.uk/news/people/father-darren-percival-bem-yorkshire-vicar-who-serves-

one-of-the-poorest-parishes-in-the-country-honoured-3717280 (accessed 28.4.23).

15 Daniel Finkelstein, 2023, 'The Secret to Happiness is Human Connection, not Economic Growth', *Times*, 24 January, at https://www. thetimes.co.uk/article/26f8626c-9c04-11ed-b81d-ce538d806950?s hareToken=faof6a8104cb274de166da17083b8725 (accessed 28.4.23).

16 See Alan Billings, 2021, 'What the Church of England Can Learn from the Police', *Church Times*, 24 September, at https://www. churchtimes.co.uk/articles/2021/24-september/comment/opinion/what-the-c-of-e-can-learn-from-the-police (accessed 28.4.23).

17 Billings, 'Learn from the Police'.

18 Billings, 'Learn from the Police'.

19 Dan Hardy, 2001, *Finding the Church: The Dynamic Truth of Anglicanism*, London: SCM Press, pp. 135–6.

20 Dan Hardy, 2010, *Wording a Radiance*, London: SCM Press, p. 53.

21 Malcolm Guite, 2018, 'Poet's Corner', *Church Times*, 2 February, at https://www.churchtimes.co.uk/articles/2018/2-february/comment/ columnists/malcolm-guite-poets-corner-real-ale-evangelism (accessed 28.4.23).

22 R. S. Thomas, 1988, 'I Was a Vicar of Large Things in a Small Parish', *The Echoes Return Slow*, London: Macmillan, p. 25.

23 David Scott, 1998, 'The Surplice', *Selected Poems*, Newcastle upon Tyne: Bloodaxe, p. 79.

Bibliography

Armstrong, Peter, 2015, 'Team Ministries in Anglican Parishes in the Maritime Provinces of Canada: Considerations for Formation and Development', PhD thesis submitted to the Faculty of Wycliffe College and the Toronto School of Theology, at https://tspace.library.utoronto.ca/bitstream/1807/69173/6/Armstrong_Peter_L_201505_DMin_thesis.pdf (accessed 28.4.23).

A Rocha, 2022, 'Stories', at https://ecochurch.arocha.org.uk/stories (accessed 28.4.23).

Atherstone, Andrew, 2022, *Repackaging Christianity: Alpha and the Building of a Global Brand*, London: Hodder and Stoughton.

Avis, Paul, 2003, *Church Drawing Near: Spirituality and Mission in a Post-Christian Culture*, London: T & T Clark.

Avis, Paul, 2007, *The Identity of Anglicanism: Essentials of Anglican Ecclesiology*, London: T & T Clark.

Barry, F. R., 1964, 'Priorities', in *The Paul Report Considered: Thirteen Essays*, ed. G. E. Duffield, Marcham Oxford: Marcham Manor Press.

Benedict XVI (Pope), 2010, 'Address to the Houses of Parliament', 17 September, at https://www.vatican.va/content/benedict-xvi/en/speeches/2010/september/documents/hf_ben-xvi_spe_20100917_societa-civile.html (accessed 28.4.23).

Bible Society, 2014, *Pass It On Report*, at https://www.biblesociety.org.uk/uploads/content/projects/Bible-Society-Report_030214_final_.pdf (accessed 28.4.23).

Billings, Alan, 2021, 'What the Church of England Can Learn from the Police', *Church Times,* 24 September, at https://www.churchtimes.co.uk/articles/2021/24-september/comment/opinion/what-the-c-of-e-can-learn-from-the-police (accessed 28.4.23).

Blöchlinger, Alex, 1965, *The Modern Parish Community*, London: Geoffrey Chapman.

Bonhoeffer, Dietrich, 1963, *Letters and Papers from Prison*, London: Fontana.

Book of Common Prayer, 1968 [1662], London: Eyre and Spottiswoode.

Brewitt-Taylor, Sam, 2018, *Christian Radicalism in the Church of England and the Invention of the British Sixties, 1957–1970: The Hope of a World Transformed*, Oxford: Oxford University Press.

Brown, A. W., 1863, *Recollections of the Conversation Parties of the Rev Charles Simeon*, London: Hamilton, Adams and Co.

Brown, Andrew, and Linda Woodhead, 2016, *That Was the Church that Was: How the Church of England Lost the English People*, London: Bloomsbury.

Bullard, J. V., 1938, *The English Parish and Diocese*, London: Faith Press.

Burnell-Nugent, James, 2022, 'Letters to the Editor', *Church Times*, 11 March.

Burns, Arthur, 1999, *The Diocesan Revival in the Church of England*, Oxford: Oxford University Press.

Bursell, Rupert, 2014, 'The Oath of Canonical Obedience', *Ecclesiastical Law Journal* 16, pp. 168–86.

Bus, Kark, Hans-Georg Becke, Eugen Ewig and Josef Vogt, 1980, *The Imperial Church from Constantine to the Early Middle Ages*, London: Burns and Oates.

Cameron, James, 2018, 'Black Metal Church Burnings: A Historical View', at https://stainedglassattitudes.wordpress.com/2018/01/13/black-metal-church-burnings-a-historical-view/ (accessed 28.4.23).

Chapman, Mark D., 2006, 'Theology in the Public Arena: The Case of South Bank Religion', in *Redefining Christian Britain: Post 1945 Perspectives,* ed. Jane Garnett, Matthew Grimley, Alana Harris, William Whyte and Sarah Williams, London: SCM Press, pp. 92–105.

Chapman, Rebecca, 2022, 'There is an Alternative to Vision and Strategy', *Church Times*, 18 November, at https://www.churchtimes.co.uk/articles/2022/18-november/comment/opinion/there-is-an-alternative-to-vision-and-strategy (accessed 28.4.23).

Church for Everyone, 2022, 'Enriched by the Farsi Community: Holy Innocents Fallowfield', at https://churchforeveryone.info/asylum-church-stories-holy-innocents (accessed 28.4.23).

Church of England, 2023, Baptism and Confirmation, at https://www.churchofengland.org/prayer-and-worship/worship-texts-and-resources/common-worship/christian-initiation/baptism-and#p168 (accessed 28.4.23).

Church of England, 2023, *Canons of the Church of England,* at https://www.churchofengland.org/about/leadership-and-governance/legal-services/canons-church-england/canons-website-edition (accessed 28.4.23).

Church of England, 2022, 'Church schools and academies', at https://www.churchofengland.org/about/education-and-schools/church-schools-and-academies (accessed 28.4.23).

Church of England, 2022, *A Consultation Document: Bishops and their ministry fit for a new context,* headed 'Confidential Briefing Prepared for The College of Bishops, September 2021', at https://www.churchtimes.co.uk/articles/2022/18-february/news/uk/bishops-and-their-ministry-full-document (accessed 28.4.23).

Church of England, 1985, *Faith in the City: The Report of the Archbishops' Commission on Urban Priority Areas*, London: Church House.

Church of England, 2022, 'Follow the Star: The Great Invitation', at https://www.churchofengland.org/media-and-news/press-releases/christmas-film-2022 (accessed 28.4.23).

Church of England, 2014, *From Anecdote to Evidence: Findings from the Church Growth Research Programme, 2011–2013*, at https://www.churchofengland.org/resources/church-growth-research-programme/anecdote-evidence (accessed 28.4.23).

Church of England, 2022, *Governance Review Update* (GS MISC 1319), at https://www.churchofengland.org/sites/default/files/2022-06/GS%20Misc%201319%20Governance%20Review_0.pdf (accessed 28.4.23).

Church of England, 2022, *Independent Report of Lowest Income Communities Funding and Strategic Funding* (the Chote Report), at https://www.churchofengland.org/sites/default/files/2022-03/IRLS%20-%20final%20report%20%282%29.pdf (accessed 28.4.23).

Church of England, 2021, *Mission in Revision: A Review of the Mission and Pastoral Measure 2011* (GS 2222), at https://www.churchofengland.org/sites/default/files/2021-06/GS%202222%20-%20Mission%20in%20Revision%20-%20A%20Review%20of%20the%20Mission%20and%20Pastoral%20Measure%202011.pdf (accessed 28.4.23).

Church of England, 2021, *Report of the Governance Review Group*, at https://www.churchofengland.org/sites/default/files/2021-09/Governance%20Review%20Group%20Report%20FOR%20PUBLICATION.pdf (accessed 28.4.23).

Church of England, 2021, *Safeguarding: Learning and Development Framework*, at https://www.churchofengland.org/sites/default/files/2021-06/SafeguardingLearningAndDevelopmentFramework2021.pdf (accessed 28.4.23).

Church of England, 2017, *Setting God's People Free: A Report from the Archbishops' Council*, at https://www.churchofengland.org/sites/default/files/2017-11/gs-2056-setting-gods-people-free.pdf (accessed 28.4.23).

Church of England, 2021, *Vision and Strategy*, at https://www.churchofengland.org/about/leadership-and-governance/emerging-church-england/vision-and-strategy (accessed 28.4.23).

Common Good Foundation, *The Plague and the Parish*, at https://togetherforthecommongood.co.uk/leading-thinkers/the-plague-and-the-parish (accessed 18.8.23).

Cottrell, Stephen, 2021, 'Commentary on *Vision and Strategy*', at https://www.churchofengland.org/sites/default/files/2021-06/A%20vision%20for%20the%20church%20of%20England%20in%20the%202020s%20-%20commentary%20by%20Stephen_Cottrell.pdf (accessed 28.4.23).

Cowling, Maurice, 1980, *Religion and Public Doctrine in Modern England*, Cambridge: Cambridge University Press.

Cragoe, Carol Davidson, 2010, 'The Custom of the English Church: Parish Church Maintenance in England before 1300', *Journal of Medieval History* 36, no. 1, pp. 20 Ð38.

Cyprian of Carthage, 1995,*On the Unity of the Church*, The Ante-Nicene Fathers, 5, eds Alexander Roberts and James Donaldson, rev. A. Cleveland Coxe, Edinburgh: T & T Clark.

Dale, Karen, 2021, *Anatomising Embodiment and Organization Theory*, Basingstoke: Palgrave.

Davies, Madeleine, 2021, 'Focal Oversight the Church of England of the Future', *Church Times*, 10 September, at https://www.churchtimes. co.uk/articles/2021/10-september/features/features/focal-oversight-the-c-of-e-of-the-future (accessed 28.4.23).

Davies, Madeleine, 2022, 'Lay Church Planters Held Back by Church Structures', *Church Times*, 25 February, at https://www.churchtimes. co.uk/articles/2022/25-february/news/uk/lay-church-planters-held-back-by-church-structures-study-suggests (accessed 28.4.23).

Davies, Madeleine, 2021, 'The Love Affair with the Parish: Has it Ended?', *Church Times*, 17 September, at https://www.churchtimes. co.uk/articles/2021/17-september/features/features/the-love-affair-with-the-parish-has-it-ended (accessed 28.4.23).

Davies, Madeleine, 2021, 'Priests and Bishops a Given in Myriad's Vision for Lay-led Churches', *Church Times*, 3 July, at https://www. churchtimes.co.uk/articles/2021/30-july/news/uk/priests-and-bishops-a-given-in-myriad-s-vision-for-lay-led-churches (accessed 28.4.23).

Davies, Madeleine, 2019, 'Revitalising Mission – But at What Cost?', *Church Times*, 22 November, at https://www.churchtimes.co.uk/ articles/2019/22-november/features/features/revitalising-mission-but-at-what-cost (accessed 28.4.23).

Davies, Madeleine, 2022, 'Salami Slicing of Ministry is Wrong', *Church Times*, 15 July, at https://www.churchtimes.co.uk/articles/2022/15-july/news/uk/salami-slicing-of-ministry-is-wrong-archbishop-of-york-tells-save-the-parish (accessed 28.4.23).

Davies, Madeleine, 2021, 'Synod to Discuss 10,000 Lay-led Churches in the Next Ten Years', *Church Times*, 2 July, at https://www.church times.co.uk/articles/2021/2-july/news/uk/synod-to-discuss-target-of-10-000-new-lay-led-churches-in-the-next-ten-years (accessed 28.4.23).

Davison, Andrew, and Alison Milbank, 2010, *For the Parish: A Critique of Fresh Expressions*, London: SCM Press.

Dinwoodie, Melville, 1968, *Religion by Radio*, London: George Allen and Unwin.

Dionysius the Areopagite, 1987, *The Celestial Hierarchy, Pseudo-Dionysius: The Complete Works*, trans. Colm Luibheid, ed. Paul Rorem, London: SPCK.

Dominiack, Paul Anthony, 2020, *Richard Hooker: The Architecture of Participation*, London: T & T Clark.

Duffield, G. E. (ed.), 1964, *The Paul Report Considered: Thirteen Essays*, Marcham, Oxford: Marcham Manor Press.

East Wivelshire, *On the Way*, Steering Group, 2022, 'Letter and Proposal of the East Wivelshire Steering Group', pdf.

Elizabeth II (Queen), 2012, 'Speech at Lambeth Palace', 15 February, at https://royal.uk/queens-speech-lambeth-palace-15-february-2012acce (accessed 28.4.23).

Elston, Vanessa, 2021, 'MAP Values at Southwark', at www.southwark.anglican.org/wp-content/uploads/2021/02/MAP-values_F.pdf (accessed 28.4.23).

Ferguson, Brian, 2020, 'Peter Howson: Artist Inspired by Catastrophe He Saw Coming', *The Scotsman*, 17 May, at https://www.scotsman.com/arts-and-culture/art/peter-howson-artist-inspired-by-catastrophe-he-saw-coming-2855764 (accessed 28.4.23).

Field, Clive, 2015, *Britain's Last Religious Revival? Quantifying Belonging, Behaving and Believing in the Long 1950s*, Basingstoke: Palgrave Macmillan.

Figgis, John Neville, 1913, *Churches in the Modern State*, London: Longmans.

Finkelstein, Daniel, 2023, 'The Secret to Happiness is Human Connection, not Economic Growth', *Times*, 24 January, at https://www.thetimes.co.uk/article/26f8626c-9c04-11ed-b81d-ce538d806950?shareToken=faof6a8104cb274de166da17083b8725 (accessed 28.4.23).

Foucault, Michel, 1977, *Discipline and Punish: The Birth of the Prison*, trans. Alan Sheridan, Harmondsworth: Penguin.

Foxe, John, 1841 [1583], *Acts and Monuments*, eds G. Townsend and S. R. Cattley, 8 vols, London: R. B. Seeley and W. Burnside.

Fresh Expressions in the Mission of the Church: Report of an Anglican–Methodist Working Party, 2012, London: Church House.

Giles, Richard, John Sadler and Robert Warren, 2020, 'Lockdown Could Change the Church Permanently', *Church Times*, 29 May, at https://www.churchtimes.co.uk/articles/2020/29-may/comment/opinion/lockdown-could-change-the-church-permanently (accessed 28.4.23).

Gregory, Jeremy, and Jeffrey Scott Chamberlain (eds), 2003, *The National Church in Local Perspective*, Woodbridge: Boydell Press.

Guder, Darrell L., and Lois Barrett, 1998, *Missional Church: A Vision for the Sending of the Church in North America*, Grand Rapids: Eerdmans.

Hake, Andrew, 1989, 'Theological Reflections on Community', in *Theology in the City: A Theological Response to 'Faith in the City'*, London: SPCK, pp. 50–52.

Hansard, 2014, HL Debate on the Importance of the English Parish Church, vol. 754, cols 542–78, 12 June, at https://hansard.parliament.

uk/lords/2014-06-12/debates/14061242000654/EnglishParish
Churches (accessed 28.4.23).

Hansard, 1976, HC Debate on Endowments and Glebe Measure, vol.
919, cols 941–6, 15 November, at https://hansard.parliament.uk/
Commons/1976-11-15/debates/290098fd-cef7-4109-ae97-
c3c6dfb44898/ChurchOfEngland(EndowMentsAndGlebeMeasure)
(accessed 28.4.23).

Hardy, Dan, 2010, *Wording a Radiance*, London: SCM Press.

Hardy, Dan, 2001, *Finding the Church: The Dynamic Truth of Anglicanism*, London: SCM Press.

Hart, A. Tindal, 1964, 'Is Saul [Paul] Among the Prophets? The Proposal
to Transform Rural Deaneries into Major Parishes with a Team', in
The Paul Report Considered: Thirteen Essays, ed. G. E. Duffield, Marcham, Oxford: Marcham Manor Press.

Hart, Ian, 1995, 'The Teaching of Luther and Calvin about Ordinary
Work', *Evangelical Quarterly* 67, no. 1, pp. 35–52.

Haynes, Nick, 2008, *Research Report on Church-State Relations in
Selected European Countries*, Edinburgh: Historic Environment Advis-
ory Council for Scotland.

Herbert, George, 1991, *The Complete English Poems*, ed. John Tobin,
London: Penguin.

Hewitt, Monica, 1964, 'A Sociological Critique', in *The Paul Report
Considered: Thirteen Essays*, ed. G. E. Duffield, Marcham, Oxford:
Marcham Manor Press.

Hill, Barry, 2021, 'Why a Mixed Ecology Matters', *Church Times*, 21
November.

Hill, Geoffrey, 1978, *Tenebrae*, London: André Deutsch.

Holland, Tom, 2019, *Dominion: The Making of the Western Mind*,
London: Little Brown.

Hooker, Richard, 1845 [1597], *Laws of Ecclesiastical Polity*, 2 vols,
Oxford: Oxford University Press.

Hull, John, 2006, *Mission-Shaped Church: A Theological Response*,
London: SCM Press.

Ignatius of Antioch, 1995, *Epistle to the Trallians, The Ante-Nicene
Fathers*, 1, eds Alexander Roberts and James Donaldson, rev. A.
Cleveland Coxe, Edinburgh: T & T Clark.

Jardat, Remi, 2007, 'How Democratic Law Leads to Low Cost Efficient
Processes', *Society and Business Review* 3, no. 1, pp. 23–40.

Jay, Elisabeth, 1979, *The Religion of the Heart: Anglican Evangelicalism and the Nineteenth Century Novel*, Oxford: Clarendon Press.

Jennings, Anthony, 2022, 'The Long Fight to Protect the Parish' at
https://savetheparish.com/2022/11/23/the-long-fight-to-protect-the-
parish-anthony-jennings/ (accessed 28.4.23).

Jeremiah, Anderson, 2021, 'Mixed Ecology Church: Why Definitions
Matter', *Church Times*, 23 July, at https://www.churchtimes.co.uk/

articles/2021/23-july/comment/opinion/mixed-ecology-church-why-definitions-matter (accessed 28.4.23).

Lang, Sean, 2000, 'A-Level History', *History Today* 50, no. 2, at https://www.historytoday.com/archive/level-history (accessed 28.4.23).

Lewis, C. S., 2012 [1952], *Mere Christianity*, London: Collins.

Lewis-Anthony, Justin, n.d., 'A Gregorian Critique of Managerialism', at https://www.academia.edu/9890319/Ecclesiastical_Bureaucracy_a_Gregorian_critique_of_Managerialism (accessed 28.4.23).

Lewis-Anthony, Justin, 2009, *If You Meet George Herbert On the Road, Kill Him: Radically Rethinking Priestly Ministry*, London: Mowbrays.

Lings, George, 2017, *Encountering the Day of Small Things*, Sheffield: Church Army.

Liverpool Diocese, 2022, *Fit for Mission*, at https://liverpool.anglican.org/making-it-easier-parishes/fitformission/led-by-local-teams/ (accessed 28.4.23).

Liverpool Diocese, 2021, *Guide to Pastoral Reorganisation*, at https://d3hgrlq6yacptf.cloudfront.net/603eb0893e402/content/pages/documents/pastoral_reorganisation_leaflet_v1.pdf (accessed 28.4.23).

MacIntyre, Alasdair, 1981, *After Virtue: A Study in Moral Theory*, London: Duckworth.

Massingham, H. J., *The Tree of Life*, Intro. Frances Hutchinson, London: Jon Carpenter, 2003 [1943].

McCormick, Felicity, 2022, 'Father Darren Percival BEM: Yorkshire Vicar who serves one of the poorest parishes in the country honoured', *Yorkshire Post*, 2 June, at www.yorkshirepost.co.uk/news (accessed 28.4.23).

McGinley, John, 2022, 'London: Gregory Centre for Church Multiplication', *Listening to the Voice of the Lay Planters*.

Mead, Loren B.,1991, *The Once and Future Church: Reinventing the Congregation for a new Mission Frontier*, New York: Alban Institute.

Milbank, Alison, 2011, 'Apologetics and the Imagination: Making Strange', in *Imaginative Apologetics: Theology, Philosophy and the Catholic Tradition*, ed. Andrew Davison, London: SCM Press, pp. 31–45.

Moon, Hawarang, 2021, 'The Influence of Liturgy on Memory: From the Perspective of Neuroscience', *Studia Liturgica* 5, no. 2, pp. 230–42.

Morris, Jeremy, 2008, *F. D. Maurice and the Crisis of Christian Authority*, Oxford: Oxford University Press.

Morris, Jeremy, 2022, *A People's Church: A History of the Church of England*, London: Profile.

Moule, H. C. G., 1892, *Charles Simeon*, London: Methuen.

Moy, Rich, 2022, 'In the Shadow of Success', at https://yournameislikehoney.com/2022/01/03/part-seventeen-in-the-shadow-of-success-5-questions-for-htb-network/ (accessed 28.4.23).

Moy, Rich, 2015, 'Men Only? A Charismatic Crisis in New Wine/ HTB Leadership', at https://yournameislikehoney.com/2015/12/05/ men-only-a-charismatic-crisis-in-new-wine-htb-leadership/ (accessed 28.4.23).

National Archives, '1951–1964 Conservative management', at www. nationalarchives.gov.uk/cabinetpapers/alevelstudies/1951-conserva tive-management.htm (accessed 28.4.23).

National Churches Trust, 2021, *The House of Good: The Economic and Social Value of Church Buildings*, at https://www.houseofgood. nationalchurchestrust.org (accessed 28.4.23).

National Churches Trust, 2018, *Visiting Churches*, at https://www. nationalchurchestrust.org/news/49-cent-british-adults-visited-church- last-year (accessed 28.4.23).

Nockles, Peter, 2008, *The Oxford Movement in Context: Anglican High Churchmanship 1760–1857*, Cambridge: Cambridge University Press.

Northcott, Michael, 2011, 'Parochial Ecology on St Briavels Common: Rebalancing the Local and the Universal in Anglican Ecclesiology and Practice', *Journal of Anglican Studies* 10, no. 1, pp. 68–93.

Noyes, James, and Phillip Blond, 2013, *Holistic Mission: Social Action and the Church of England*, Lincoln: ResPublica.

O'Donovan, Oliver, 2005, *Ways of Judgment*, Grand Rapids MI: Eerd- mans.

O'Loughlin, Thomas, 2015, *Washing Feet: Imitating the Example of Jesus in the Liturgy Today*, Collegeville MN: Liturgical Press.

Orme, Nicholas, 2021, *Going to Church in Medieval England*, New Haven CT: Yale University Press.

Parish Nursing, 2022, 'Autumn Newsletter of Parish Church Ministries', at https://parishnursing.org.uk/news/ (accessed 28.4.23).

Pattison, Stephen, 1997, *The Faith of the Managers*, New York: Con- tinuum.

Paul, Ian, 2019, 'What Are the Issues in Ministerial Training?' at https:// www.psephizo.com/life-ministry/what-are-the-issues-in-ministerial- training/ (accessed 28.4.23).

Paul, Ian, 2020, 'What Is Happening to the Church of England?' at https:// www.psephizo.com/life-ministry/what-is-happening-to-church- of-england-attendance/ (accessed 28.4.23).

Paul, Leslie, 1964, *The Deployment and Payment of the Clergy*, London: Church Information Office.

Payne, Martin, 2015, 'A Year in the Life of One Messy Church', at https://www.messychurch.org.uk/messy-blog/year-life-one-messy- church (accessed 28.4.23).

Penduck, Joshua, 2017, 'The Week Evangelicals Began to Take Over the Church of England', 6 March, at https://openevangelical. wordpress.com/2017/03/06/the-week-evangelicals-began-to-take- over-the-church-of-england/ (accessed 28.4.23).

Percy, Martin, 1997, 'Consecrated Pragmatism', *Anvil* 14, no. 1, pp. 18–25.

Percy, Martyn, 2012, *The Ecclesial Canopy: Faith, Hope and Charity*, Farnham: Ashgate.

Percy, Martyn, 2021, 'The Great Leap Forward Part One: The New Politics of Ecclesionomics for the Church of England', at https://modernchurch.org.uk/martyn-percy-the-great-leap-forward-part-one-the-new-politics-of-ecclesionomics-for-the-church-of-england (accessed 28.4.23).

Percy, Martyn, 2017, 'How George Bell Became a Victim of Church of England Spin and Decisive Leadership', Archbishop Cranmer blog, at https://archbishopcranmer.com/bishop-george-bell-victim-church-england-spin-narrative-decisive-leadership/ (accessed 28.4.23).

Percy, Martyn, 2022, 'Some Critical Comments on "Bishops and Ministry Fit for a New Context"', at https://anglican.ink/2022/02/21/martyn-percy-some-critical-comment-on-bishops-and-ministry-fit-for-a-new-context/ (accessed 28.4.23).

Percy, Martyn, 2019, '"Your Church Can Grow!" – A Contextual Theological Critique of Megachurches', in *Handbook of Megachurches*, ed. Stephen Hunt, Leiden: Brill, pp. 103–27.

Podmore, Colin, 2006, 'The Church of England's Understanding of Episcopacy', *Theology* 109, no. 849, pp. 173–81.

Putnam, 2001, *Bowling Alone: the Collapse and Revival of American Community*, New York: Simon and Schuster.

Quiggin, John, 2003, 'Word for Wednesday: Managerialism', at https://johnquiggin.com/2003/07/02/word-for-wednesday-managerialism-definition/ (accessed 28.4.23).

Ramsay, Christopher, 1995, 'Nineteenth Century Urbanization and the Church of England: An Assessment', at www.Anglicanism.org (accessed 28.4.23).

Rich, Hannah, 2020, *Growing Good: Growth, Social Action and Discipleship in the Church of England*, London: Theos, 2020, pp. 12–14, at https://cuf.org.uk/uploads/resources/CUF-GRACE-Report-2020.pdf (accessed 28.4.23).

Robinson, John, 1974 [1963], *Honest to God*, London: SCM Press.

Robinson, Thomas A, 2016, *Who Were the First Christians? Dismantling the Urban Thesis*, Oxford: Oxford University Press.

Robinson, Tiffer, 2022, 'Saving the Parish is Possible', at https://savetheparish.com/2022/04/26/saving-the-parish-is-possible-rev-canon-tiffer-robinson/ (accessed 28.4.23).

Roman Catholic Church, 1983, Canon 368, *Code of Canon Law*, at https://www.vatican.va/archive/cod-iuris-canonici/eng/documents/cic_lib2-cann368-430_en.html#SECTION_II._PARTICULAR_CHURCHES_AND_THEIR_GROUPINGS (accessed 28.4.23).

Rumsey, Andrew, 2017, *Parish: An Anglican Theology of Place*, London: SCM Press.

Save the Parish, 2022, 'Parish Christmas Stories', at https://savethepar ish.com/2022/12/21/parishes-at-christmas-various (accessed 28.4.23).

Scott, David, 1998, *Selected Poems*, Newcastle upon Tyne: Bloodaxe.

Shakespeare, Lyndon, 2016, *Being the Body of Christ in an Age of Management*, Eugene OR: Cascade.

Shillitoe, Rachel, 2020, 'Evaluation Study of Understanding Christianity', at https://www.understandingchristianity.org.uk/the-project/ project-evaluation-understanding-christianity/ (accessed 28.4.23).

Skinner, S. A., 2004, *Tractarians and the Condition of England: The Social and Political Thought of the Oxford Movement*, Oxford: Clarendon Press.

Syke Community Church interview, 2022, at Antioch Network, Diocese of Manchester at https://www.antiochnetwork.org.uk/syke-commu nity-church (accessed 28.4.23).

Temple, William, 1928, *Christianity and the State*, London: Macmillan.

Thomas, Edward, 1975, *Poems of Edward Thomas*, intro. Walter de la Mare, Oxford: Oxford University Press.

Thomas, R. S., 1988, *The Echoes Return Slow*, London: Macmillan.

Thompson, Kenneth, 1975, 'Church House and Margaret Parkes', *Astonishing Good Fortune*, Loughborough: West and Lissaman.

Thorlby, Tim, 2016, *Love, Sweat and Tears: Church Growth in East London*, London: Centre for Theology and Community.

Thorlby, Tim, 2017, *A Time to Sow: Anglican Catholic Church Growth in London*, London: Centre for Theology and Community.

Tilby, Angela, 2022, 'Bishops' Unanimity is Shameful', *Church Times*, 4 March, at https://www.churchtimes.co.uk/articles/2022/4-march/ comment/columnists/angela-tilby-bishops-unanimity-is-shameful (accessed 28.4.23).

Tilby, Angela, 2021, 'Ministry that is Lay-Led is not Anglican', *Church Times*, 8 October, at https://www.churchtimes.co.uk/articles/2021/ 8-october/comment/columnists/angela-tilby-ministry-that-is-lay-led- is-not-anglican (accessed 28.4.23).

Treacy, Eric, 1964, 'Approaching the Report', in *The Paul Report Considered: Thirteen Essays*, ed. G. E. Duffield, Marcham, Oxford: Marcham Manor Press.

Trinity College Bristol, 2022, blog, at https://www.trinitycollegebristol. ac.uk/blog/kingdom-learning/new-class-on-bonhoeffer/ (accessed 28.4.23).

Tweedie, Fiona, 2016, *Going Deeper, Church Attendance Statistics and Clergy Deployment*, at https://www.churchofengland.org/sites/ default/files/2020-01/going_deeper_final_0.pdf (accessed 28.4.23).

Vaughan, Henry, 1914, *The Works of Henry Vaughan*, 2 vols, ed. Leonard Cyril Martin, Oxford: Clarendon Press.

Vickers, Clare, et al., 2022, Letters, *Church Times*, 18 March, at https://www.churchtimes.co.uk/articles/2022/18-march/comment/letters-to-the-editor/letters-to-the-editor (accessed 28.4.23).

Weil, Simone, 2008 [1949], *The Need for Roots: Prelude to a Declaration of Duties Towards Mankind*, trans. Arthur Wills, London: Routledge.

'Wigan Representations to the Church Commissioners', 2019, formerly, now removed, at https://www.churchofengland.org/resources/church-growth-research-programme/anecdote-evidence 9 (accessed 28.4.23).

Index of Names and Subjects